She's Bearing All Fruits

If you don't like the harvest you are reaping, check the seeds you are sowing.

By
LaDwina Flegeance

She's Bearing All Fruits
One Housewife's Journey to Find an Abundant Life Through Love, Self-Empowerment, and Faith

Copyright ©2023 LADWINA FLEGEANCE. All rights reserved.

No part of this book may be reproduced in any form or by any mechanical means, including information storage and retrieval systems without permission in writing from the publisher or author, except by a reviewer who may quote passages in a review. All images, logos, quotes, and trademarks included in this book are subject to use according to trademark and copyright laws of the United States of America.

FLEGEANCE, LADWINA, Author
SHE'S BEARING ALL FRUITS
LADWINA FLEGEANCE

Published by
ELITE ONLINE PUBLISHING
63 East 11400 South
Suite #230
Sandy, UT 84070
EliteOnlinePublishing.com

ISBN: 978-1-956642-62-9 (eBook)
ISBN: 978-1-956642-61-2 (Paperback)

BIO018000
REL012120

QUANTITY PURCHASES: Schools, companies, professional groups, clubs, and other organizations may qualify for special terms when ordering quantities of this title. For information, email info@eliteonlinepublishing.com.

All rights reserved by LADWINA FLEGEANCE and ELITE ONLINE PUBLISHING
This book is printed in the United States of America.

Praise for LaDwina Flegeance

Have you ever felt like there's more to life? In "She's Bearing All Fruits," LaDwina shares how life should be worth living for, not just existing. I'm confident her story will relate to women of all ages. You will be inspired to live your life purposefully without any regrets. Planting good in people will always bring a harvest to enjoy in any season of your life.

LaKisha Milson
First Lady of First Holy Ghost C.O.G.I.C.

LaDwina spoke many things my heart speaks. As wives, mothers, and women of God, we forget to live life on purpose because we become comfortable. She is definitely bearing fruits with words of wisdom and encouragement. This book has blessed me with hard truths to live by.

Anika F Porter, M.Ed
Speaker, Author, Consultant, and Founder of APorter Books

This insightful, provoking read will empower everyday people to achieve success while gleaning nuggets of truth from the author's wisdom. This book is filled with real-life wisdom and reflection to propel women to bear the fruit through the timeless truth!

Dr. Warren Milson, III
Senior Pastor of FHG Church and
Christ Community Church, Author of Grace Leadership

Dedication

This book is for the woman who has committed to her daily journey of living a fruitful life outside the four walls of her home.

Foreword

You will be tremendously blessed once you embark on this journey of freedom. The practical application and delivery have opened my eyes to a higher calling and purpose for my life. They have inspired me to move forward, creating a paradigm shift in my spirit and soul to a higher purpose of living. I can assure you that "She's Bearing All Fruits" will bring you out of your cocoon and allow you to blossom into a beautiful butterfly. The author desires you to become fruitful as God designed you to be. We all have a uniqueness about us; as the author mentioned in the book, we are all beautiful flowers in different colors.

LaDwina's goals are to remind you of the sweet smell of the flowers and to help you understand that life has storms that may diminish your spirit, and cause some part of your purpose to wither away. But, however big the storm, she concludes you must be planted in order to grow. Her linguistic use of the fruit of the spirit written by Paul to the Church of Galatians reminds me of parallels to other great speakers whose dynamic and practical everyday life scenarios penetrate our hearts and minds through our television and radio stations across the country.

LaDwina's style and contrast of the fruit of the spirit are similar, encouraging in the direction of Joyce Meyer, Joni Eareckson Tada, and Priscilla Shirer. All of whom inspirational leadership has helped us to live in this new culture with style and grace.

I have had the pleasure to see LaDwina go through the things she mentioned in the book, and it is my pleasure even to have participated in all these phases of her life. She has manifested these fruits in her everyday life with family and colleagues alike.

Unlike cake ingredients which are nasty on their own but, when mixed, make the perfect blend. According to Paul, the fruit of the spirit is one fruit with all these ingredients. Nevertheless, each one can stand on its own because they represent the character of Christ's likeness.

The author Christ's characteristics reveal themselves in the way she leads from the beginning

FOREWORD

of the introduction to the very end. With "The Fear of the Lord" and her personal commentary on a Proverbs 31 woman.

When we read the wisdom literature of the bible," *Proverbs*," the book opens its first few verses with the secret to wisdom and knowledge.

Proverbs 1:5 (NIV) says, Let the wise listen and add to their learning, and let the discerning get guidance."

Proverbs 1:7 (NIV)The fear of the Lord is the beginning of knowledge...

"She's Bearing All Fruits" is the desire of the author to pour out her Christ-likeness on you, the reader.

Sometimes, you will feel doubt, and guilt will creep into your purpose, but the author gives you seeds of affirmation and encouragement to live your life more abundantly.

Seeds are buried deep into the ground. Before it can grow, it has to be watered. When emotional storms of life come, the author echoes that these storms are only the water needed to grow. You have to be planted to rise again.

When reading this book, I do not only see a book for early educators desiring to be inspired in their new careers or a seasoned educator questioning their purpose. However, this book would be the perfect part of their preparation.

I have been a business owner for over two decades, worked with several fortune five hundred companies, and have been part of several church planting. This book application can be applied to any career: any campaign and organization.

It inspires, empowers, and encourages change that is uncomfortable but needed. It gives individuals, teams, families, corporations, and associations a self-fulfilling purpose.

John Piper, an American theologian, says," Our goal in life should not be to stay alive but to live life until the course has run out." But, of course, his disposition is God's purpose for your life.

You may have questions regarding your existence. Like Adonis Creed fictional character from the Rocky film series, one of the movie's best lines is when Rocky asks him, "Why are you doing this" he answers, "I want to prove I wasn't a mistake." Once he found his purpose, it fueled his fire and his desire to be a champion. I am not sure what your purpose is, but God speaks to us in three ways. Through his word, through his spirit, and through other people.

I pray for you to be blessed and inspired by the words of this book like I have.

Donavon Flegeance
President of D.R.I.V.E. International Outreach
Author of *Reality Check: Exploring the Sci-Fiction From A Biblical Point Of View* and *Bold: From The Agora To The Areopagus.*

She's Forever Bearing Fruits.

She's Bearing all Fruits is based on the noble character of the woman of Proverbs 31 and the attributes of the fruit of the spirit *(love, joy, peace, patience, kindness, goodness, faithfulness, gentleness, and self-control)*.

This book is about the author's journey from being a stay-at-home housewife to ultimately taking the courage to walk in her purpose outside the walls of her home. Her passion started as a teacher in education, to a small business owner, and now an advocate for women's success. Her journey has opened doors for many other women to be confident within themselves to succeed and conquer greatness. Regardless of your status or career, you, too, can implement your journey into this story.

This book is intended to inspire, enlighten, and motivate others on their journey called life. It will initiate reflections on life decisions and career paths and help the reader create a road map for their journey to self-awareness and how their life impacts others around them.

Inspired by many other women empowerment stories, She's Bearing ALL Fruits captures all the essentials of a fruitful life.

Special Thanks

Thank you, God, for showing me the life path and how to embrace my calling.

Thank you to my husband, Donavon, my childhood best friend, for your never-ending love and encouragement throughout our marriage.

Thank you to my children, Daylon and Destiny, for allowing me to be your mom.

Thank you to my sisters, LaKisha and LaTyra, for being the best sisters any girl could ask for. Our sister bond will forever be cherished, even beyond death.

Thank you, to my girlfriends and fellow housewives, for the many empowerment stories, laughs, and love you have given me throughout my journey.

Table of Contents

Introduction xix

Chapter 1: **LOVE** life. Live for your Purpose. 3

Chapter 2: No plan. No worries. There's still **JOY**. 23

Chapter 3: The Visit. **PEACE** be unto you. 43

Chapter 4: Have **PATIENCE.** And you will reap the benefits.. 61

Chapter 5: Dress for Success. Clothed yourself with **KINDNESS.** 91

Chapter 6: Move On. **GOODNESS** and Mercy will follow you. 107

Chapter 7: Sister Talk. **FAITHFULNESS** to inspire others. 123

Chapter 8: **GENTLENESS** will lead to Greatness.. 143

Chapter 9: **SELF-CONTROL** = Awareness + Reflection. .159

Chapter 10: You are **FRUITFUL.**. 173

Conclusion 183

She's Bearing All Fruits Highlights 187

Endnotes 193

About the Author 195

Introduction:

Her Story

The woman who is worthy of praise is not necessarily the one, who does all her own housework or is a natural in beauty — but the woman who fears the Lord is to be praised.

Beauty, power, and wealth lie within the most successful businesswoman. She is gifted with many talents for navigating through challenging decision-making and demonstrates leadership skills. She is envied by many while loved by most. Her charismatic personality enlightens those who surround her. She wears different hats daily: mom, wife, sister, daughter, friend, entrepreneur, author, etc., to name a few. Her strength overshadows her weakness and is a mighty force to be reckoned with. Her heroic powers lie deep within, making her fearless of those with evil doings. She is the most bonafide woman known to walk in her purpose without any regrets. While standing tall in her confidence, she flourishes with the best powerful seeds given to her. She produces love, joy, peace, patience, kindness, goodness, faithfulness, greatness, and self-control. She is forever sowing fruitfulness into the lives of others. One may ask, where can this woman be found? Who is she? To see her, you must be willing to take this journey of self-discovery, unleashing your true character. You must be ready to take on new opportunities that will come your way. And when you do, you will find her rooted deep inside you.

With more than 50 women cited in the Bible, their characters range from a parade of prostitutes, evil queens, prophetesses, wealthy women, abused women, single and married women, and widows, young and old. These women are intentionally mentioned in the Bible for their extraordinary acts.

To name a few of my favorites: Abigail, the wife of David, was a generous, quick-witted, and wise woman. She is one of the Bible's greatest peacemakers.

Next, there's Deborah, a world leader whose vision of the world was shaped not by the political situations of her day but by her relationship with God. Though women in the ancient world did not usually become political leaders, Deborah was just the leader Israel needed. And one of my last but not least favorites was Lydia, a widowed mother. She was a successful businesswoman known for selling prized purple-color garments. As head of her household, she had a firm faith, and her entire family followed her example and was baptized.

These are just a few examples of many women's lifestyles in the Bible. These women all have one thing in common: they are real women who struggle with their self-awareness and risk their lives and reputations for the sake of others. Though our culture differs from theirs, we still share just as many of their emotional responses and concerns. These women are a testimony to what every woman may endure daily. Their stories are forever etched in stone as enlightenment for other women who walked a similar journey as theirs. They all had lived purposeful lives. But compared to one woman, whose story is put on a pedestal of praise by her husband and children. She was accredited for her wisdom and known for her behavior of showing high moral standards.

Who is she?

She is the woman in Proverbs 31. A woman who was capable, intelligent, and virtuous. She was a mother to her children and a wife to her husband. "Her children arise and call her blessed. Her husband also praises her, saying, 'Many women do noble things, but you surpass them all'" [1]. She is a wife of noble character that represents the fulfillment of a life lived in wisdom. Yet, she chose the knowledge of God over the understanding of the world. She was a woman worthy of praise not so much for doing her house chores or her natural beauty, but she was a woman who received recognition because she feared the Lord Almighty.

Proverbs is a practical handbook for leading a life based on wisdom. In Proverbs 31:30, it becomes clear that the "reverent and worship fear of the Lord," which is "the beginning of wisdom," is the proper foundation for a life that God values.

The woman of Proverbs 31 was meant to inspire others with a picture of what a virtuous life can produce: shelter for others, serenity, honor, prosperity, generosity, confidence about the future, and true fruitfulness.

Today, many women question their calling and purpose besides being a mother, wife, sister,

---

[1] Book of Proverbs 31:28-29

or daughter. They sometimes find themselves in a complacent state of unawareness, not knowing which direction of life they want to go in. Therefore, they cannot truly fulfill their identity and self-discovery. They ask themselves: How can I feel USEFUL to others outside my duties? What is my purpose in life? What role do I play in this society that will benefit others? Many women circle these questions regarding their life's path or their purpose for existing. They long for any signs of affirmation from others to help them discover their function in life.

The most profound question that most women ask God is, "*What do YOU want me to do, Lord?*" Leads up to the next question and thought: "*What is my calling, and how do I answer that call?*"

For you to hear the voice of God, you must have an open heart of obedience to want to do HIS will. God is a God who works all things, including your life, according to His purposes. Nothing can happen without God ordaining it. If you are truly ready to live a life of excitement that rewards others and yourself, go to God in prayer, dig deeper into His word, and determine your gifts, strength, and passion. Put your prayer into action and surround yourself with people who will serve as your counselor (advisory team) to help you find God's purpose and call for you.

Just as the woman in Proverbs 31 adhered to God's voice, she was praised for her obedience to fear the Lord. His voice and comfort gave her confidence to know she was worthy. She didn't hide in her home doing the mundane routine of daily household work. Instead, she was known for other noble things done outside her home. She had excelled with many women listed in the bible. Her exceptional level went beyond the works of *Miriam*, the one who led a nation's women in praise to God (Exodus 15:20,21); *Ruth*, the woman of constancy (Ruth 1:16); *Hannah*, the ideal mother (1 Samuel 1:20; 2:19); *the Shunammite*, the hospitable woman (2 Kings 4:8-10); *Huldah*, the woman who revealed God's secret message to national leaders (2 Kings 22:14); and even more than *Queen Esther*, the woman who risked sacrificing her life for her people (Esther 4:16). In what way did she, the woman of Proverbs 31 "excel them all"? Her spiritual and practical devotion to God permeated every area and relationship of her life. She displayed all seven Christian virtues (humility, charity, chastity, gratitude, temperance, patience, and diligence)[2]. Her secret, which is open to everyone, is the Holy Spirit's climax to the story and this book. She knew her purpose in life and laughed at the days to come.

Many might say she's a fictional character from an Old Testament bible story. But is she? Her name is not mentioned in the Bible, but does that not make her relevant to women today? She took care of her household..." arose while it was still dark to feed her family. She looked at a field, considered its merits, and purchased it. She wove cloth and made lien garments, which she then sold"[3]. This sounds like a woman many can relate to, including me. Most women take care of their household's necessities by waking up early to prepare breakfast for the kids, husband, or even family members who might live in the house. Then off to work or out to their daily routines. The woman of Proverbs 31 may have been generations long before our time, but she is still a relevant woman of today's age. But what makes her stand out even more, is that

---

[2] Seven Christian virtues (2 Peter 1:5)
[3] Book of Proverbs 31:15-24

she is a woman that fears the Lord. She knew who to rely on for strength and gave thanks and praise.

In this world, numerous successful business women are uplifting and a blessing to many others. This is because their great deeds go far beyond what is expected of them. And because of their remarkable deeds, they will always be remembered.

In this self-discovery journey, you will learn to embrace the woman God has called you to be. A woman who will walk in wisdom, knowing the truth of her existence. You will live a life of service that will be gratifying to others, sowing seeds that will harvest a lifetime of fruitfulness.

This book gives you the basic foundations needed to live a fruitful life. Those fundamental principles will help you reflect on how you choose to live a bountiful life. By applying these methods, you will begin to live a life of merits that will forever be remembered, impacting so many lives around you and generations to come.

My Story

(Part 1: Self-Awareness)

It's New Year's Eve, and I have sought to find my "one" word for the coming new year. In my culture, it is tradition to come up with a New Year's resolution each year. A New Year's resolution is a promise you make to yourself at the beginning of the year to start doing something good or stop doing something wrong. This time, instead of focusing on a particular deed, I wanted to focus on one specific word to help me discover who God called me to be. In the past, I have used words like "perseverance," *the ability to do something despite difficulty or delay in achieving success*. I have also used "resilience," *the ability to recover quickly or bounce back from problems*. Both words brought meaning to my life and helped me achieve what I had set out to do. But this year, I wanted a new word that was not trending on social media. Instead, I wanted a word that would speak to me and make me dig deep into who I wanted to become. A word that speaks life. This word would define the woman I was meant to live out, not just for this new year but for all the recent years.

Today was the last day of the year, and I woke up feeling the need to give God all the praise and glory, for HE has been so good to my family and me this year and all the years that have passed. I had an intense urge to read my Bible and to reflect on God's word. It was like God was tugging on my heart, forcing me to stop and listen to HIS voice. For the most part, I would read my Bible daily, but lately, I have been neglecting my devotional time due to busyness with other things. I had let the chaos of life consume the Bible reading time that I had initially allotted as a part of my daily routine. Now that I was searching for my "one" word for the year, I wanted to spend some extra personal time with God in hopes of guidance to seek the word I was looking for. The book of Matthew, chapter 7, states, "if you ask, then it shall be given to you; seek, and you shall find...." That morning, I was looking for an answer in the form of a word.

MY STORY

As I picked up my Bible, I felt God's peace and a sense of joy as I started to embrace HIS word. Then, I began reading Galatians, an epistle written by the Apostle Paul to the church in Galatia. The letter of Galatians is the ninth book of the New Testament, which only has six chapters. It is a short read, and its content is reasonably understandable. Suppose you would like to start taking part in reading daily scriptures. Then I would highly encourage you to start with the book of Galatians.

I have found that reading the Bible is the best way to develop a relationship with God. It will open your heart and mind to dig deeper into God's words. Words that will bring comfort and prosperity over your life. That morning, it was imperative that I just didn't read the Bible out of obligation but to dig deeper into hearing HIS voice. I wanted God to know I was open to hearing the word HE had set for me that day.

As I continued reading the Galatians letter, I began to self-reflect on how I fit in today's society and what role I played. I keep coming across the word "Love." I didn't consider "love" my one word, but I didn't want to send the wrong message if I had to pick that word. I didn't want people to think I couldn't love or show affection affiliated with the word love. Sometimes other people's perceptions can cause wavering doubts in one's mind. I know I shouldn't care what others think if I choose that word. However, I needed my one word to be a little more persistent, and "love," wasn't it. At least, that's what I thought at the time.

As I read deeper into the book, the word love led me to the word "Fruit." Chapter 5, verse 22 in the book of Galatians states… *"but the fruit of the spirit is love."* Pondering on that verse really opened my heart, mind & soul. When you think of a fruit, you think of the sweetness and goodness it gives your body. The nutrient that provides nourishment essential for growth and the maintenance of life. In searching for my one word, not knowing, I was searching for a life that would produce the goodness of God's love. So, in that aha moment, I defined my one word for the new year, "**Fruitful**," *the ability to show love, joy, peace, patience, kindness, goodness, faithfulness, gentleness, and self-control.*

In discovering the word fruitful, God let me know HE wanted me to be productive throughout my life and not just for that year. HE wanted me to be aware of the harvest I was reaping and the seeds I needed to sow in my life and into the lives of others. HE saw greatness and productivity in me, which I couldn't see at the time. And because of HIM, I was now able to discover my purpose. It was time for me to live out my calling, bearing all the fruits one can hold.

My Story Continues
(Part 2: Self-Reflection)

Candy Land was one of my favorite board games as a child. It was a classic game where players chose a colored gingerbread man piece and would move it along a multi-colored pathway toward the game-winning objective of Candy Castle. Along the way, you might get to visit unique locations like Gum Drop Mountain and Candy Cane Forest, or you might get to meet memorable characters such as Princess Forstine and Gramma Nutt.

What I liked most about this game is that it was very colorful and had yummy treats that reminded you of how sweet and lovely things can be. Every pathway was enticing, full of fun adventures with sweet treats and friendly fictional characters along the way.

Speaking of fun adventures, another great classic of mine is the movie, The Wizard of Oz. The Wizard of Oz was more than just a girl trying to find her way back home; it was about choosing the right path and guidance to help her get there. Both classics demonstrate a synopsis of pathways one would have traveled down before. Whether it's the sweet life of happiness or the darkness of despair, God has predestined a path for your life. It's up to you what route you choose; your choices and actions play a vital role when discovering your purpose and heeding your calling.

Growing up in the boondocks, a small town with less than 100 people living there, gave me little to do or see. The lack of excitement about being there led me to imagine a world bigger than my eyes could perceive. I knew it had to be more to this world than just this countryside of living. Just like the game Candy Land and the movie, The Wizard of Oz, I, too, was hoping for a magical road that would lead me to a destination where life was full of colorful moments and promising opportunities. Nothing wrong with living a country lifestyle and enjoying nature. But being young, I didn't want to limit my potential to live a purposeful life based on the size of my town. I had envisioned myself living in a big city as one of the following three: a doctor, a teacher, or an entrepreneur. I wanted my life to be impactful to so many other people outside my circle. My motto was If I can think it, then I can see it. If I can see it, then I can live it.

As a young adolescent maturing into adulthood, I wanted to live a life that would inspire others. Not knowing the ups and downs I would face, I still envisioned living a great life. I had big dreams, goals, and aspirations that I was willing to achieve someday. I was blessed to have the title of a daughter, sister, wife, and mother. All of which any woman would have dreamed of. My life was constantly transforming into many stages that brought many happy memorable moments that will forever be cherished. Living a good life was all good, but I realized my life had a more significant meaning than just living well. I had to self-reflect on what I was doing to make it great. I had to ask myself, what was I giving and not just receiving from life that made it so enjoyable?

As I reflected on that question, I noticed I was only receiving the fruits of others' labor and nothing from my work. I had yet to sow any of my seeds leading to this point in my life. Even though I had those many titles listed above, it still didn't reflect who I was. I had yet to start walking into a life I once envisioned as a young adult. A life that would inspire and impact those around me, my community, and the world.

There will be moments in your life where you will find yourself in public places of contentment, or you may find yourself in public places that are not pleasing to your life. Those places can sometimes keep you trapped in thinking this is what your life is supposed to be. When those situational circumstances take hold of your life, it's time to self-reflect on how to obtain your purpose. If you are constantly living in a harvest where you are only gaining and not producing, you are robbing yourself of a fruitful life. **If you don't like the harvest you are currently in, then maybe it's time to check the seeds you are sowing**.

In this book, you will discover that your life is worth more than what you have subjected it to be. In addition, you will become aware of the harvest you are currently in and how your life decisions impact those around you.

With prayer and reflection, you will have a clear path to your purpose and calling. By the time you finish reading this book, you will have created a road map with the correct coordinates that will lead you to a fruitful life. Your choices in picking the right seeds to sow will be based on the will of God. Your obedience to God's voice will make you a great, faithful servant. You will walk in confidence, wisdom, and boldness, knowing you are a genuine woman of faith called by God. Your current title that you hold will be worth more than what it was in the past. Your story will be empowering and imprinted in the hearts of so many other women. Your willingness to start this journey is the first step to discovering what harvest you are in.

Are you ready?

Let's begin.

Love

The First Fruit

Chapter 1:

LOVE life. Live for your purpose.

"You can give without loving, but you cannot love without giving." — Victor Hugo

Live, Laugh, and Love is a familiar phrase printed on a canvas on my kitchen counter. These words can be found in many homes worldwide, displayed on mantels, picture frames, desktops, and even embroidered on different types of clothing. It symbolizes how we should embrace life and live in every moment. When you express laughter every day, it can produce positive emotions that lead to an entire and happy life. These feelings – like *amusement, happiness, delight, and joy* – build resiliency and increase creative thinking in one's being. When you love beyond words, you express a connection that only actions can speak. Many people have expressed their love through gifts, quality time, words of affirmation, acts of service, and physical touch[4]. Living, laughing, and loving are more than words; it is a declaration of how your life should be.

Growing up as a child, you think about life as an adult. What the future may look like or how many kids you may want. You imagine how your spouse will be and if he will be the perfect one. You even think about the place and geographic location of where you want to live. You dream big dreams about your future and what it will take to get you there. This imagination is a life that any child might envision. Thinking of living the ideal life is normal and part of human nature.

As for me, growing up in a tiny town in Louisiana where the next grocery store was about 20 miles away. I lived on a small farm with my parents and two sisters at the time. Growing up in a rural area makes you think about the world and what's out there besides sugar cane fields, chicken coops, horses & pig pens. It makes you reflect on life and your purpose for living on this earth. Rick Warren wrote the book called *"The Purpose Driven Life."* The book discusses your

---

[4] Gary Chapman, The Five Love Language

life purpose and what you should do while on earth.

As I grew in age, my reasoning for living became more defined. I knew I wanted to help others accomplish their goals, dreams, and aspirations. By doing so, I wanted to become a teacher who would change the trajectory of another's life by acquiring knowledge and competence. I wanted to contribute to education, not just be another highly educated woman who thinks she knows everything. But I also had other dreams; I wanted to be a doctor, entrepreneur, and woman of empowerment. Of course, you dream of everything you can be or do when you are young. But, you may ask how a teacher, doctor, and entrepreneur all fit in or tie into each other. Well, one thing is sure: all three institutions have a common factor: serving others.

I started journaling at an early age in life. I would write down my reflection on the day and how I would change certain decisions if given the opportunity. I would also write down things I wanted to try in life. Hoping one day, I will live long enough to accomplish all the items on my "bucket list." A bucket list is several experiences or achievements a person hopes to have or accomplish during their lifetime. Being young with a long bucket list, I was determined to fulfill every item. However, I realized I couldn't do anything on the list unless I discovered who I was. I had to find out what I wanted out of life, but most importantly, what I was willing to give in life. To achieve fulfillment, you must be aware of your gives and takes. You must begin with the things that will help you fulfill your goals and define your purpose on why you exist. Those things are the central motivations for your life. For me, I wanted to be more aware of what those things were.

I wanted to know exactly what defines a person's purpose in life. I wasn't sure if it was motivation, reasoning, or functionality. Or if it was a desire to accomplish something bigger than self. Being a kid, thinking about why I existed was very perplexing. All I knew was that my life's meaning had to be bigger than what I was accustomed to living. I knew that one day I wanted to be a part of something that would significantly impact the lives of others. But before I could influence others, I had to define my purpose.

When you are young, the people who surround you, like your family members, will be the people who will guide you in helping you find your

THE FIRST FRUIT

purpose. My mom played an important part in guiding me in my spiritual journey. She would read the Bible to my sisters and me and take us to weekly Sunday school services. There, at the children's church, is where I accepted Christ at a young age. Accepting Christ's love brought awareness of why I had existed in life. I knew I was created to live a life that was pleasing to HIM. A life that was full of love and compassion for HIS people. Because of the love of Christ my mother had bestowed in my life, now, I could display that same love in the lives of other people who surrounded me.

Understanding Christ's love, known as "agape" love, is the first sign of self-love. Having that self-love will lead to self-awareness which will help to unlock your purpose and gifts in life. This type of love is accessible at no cost. You just have to be willing to accept it. Once you are ready to bear on this first fruit, you can define how you want to express it to yourself and others. Expressing your love to others will usually come in some form of action.

In most cases, if not all, when you love something, you are more vulnerable to showing it. You think about its enjoyment and then act

LOVE

on that joy. Your thoughts and actions generate from a cognitive state of mind, producing a firm decision one will make. Therefore, when you love, it is a mental action, it will not be passive, but instead, it will be assertive. It is an assurance, a pledge, a vow of one's ability that is easily free from self-doubt or uncertainty. And one of the most significant ways most people express their love is through giving.

Winston S. Churchill says, "We make a living by what we get. We make a life by what we give." Thinking if this statement is true or not. Giving is a part of life and how living is defined. Giving can also express or instill gratitude, whether you are on the giving or receiving end; this gratitude is essential to happiness, health, and social bonds. It is in our human nature to contribute and to give. God created us to be a life of givers. Givers are willing to share daily without any strings attached to it. Those who give abundance, whether providing food, clothes, money, time, or advice, are sowing seeds of love in a more profound way that cannot be measured or quantifiable. When discovering your life purpose, you must know what you are willing to give. It can be something physical and or emotional. Making life decisions will be based on the type of love you are ready to give. If you give your life to serve others, God will give you more life to live and enjoy.

When I married my husband and had kids, my greatest affection was to be the best wife and mom I could be. I poured all my heart into serving my family, putting their needs as a top priority, if not equal to mine. I loved spending every opportunity we had together, especially our family vacations. Our family vacation getaways were the best quality time spent, and the memories will forever be priceless. In those moments of expressing my love to my family, I didn't realize that "quality time" was a type of love language I had enjoyed showing the most. At the time, I was unaware of the different kinds of love languages perceived by others. Sometimes, it can be difficult for a person to express their love when they are unsure how to show it. Those defined love languages helped me learn how I enjoy giving and receiving love. You can express your love to others better by identifying your love language. Doing so will create a more profound love connection towards others that will not fade away. For me, having quality time with my family showed that my focus was center point just on their needs and attention.

It also showed that I cared deeply about their well-being, which brought great joy to my soul. Because I was eager to know more about my love language, I took the Love Language quiz to learn other ways to express my love toward others. After taking the quiz and receiving my scores, I wasn't surprised by my results. I scored high in quality time, receiving/giving gifts, and acts of service. These were the areas where I had enjoyed expressing my love before learning about the Love Language quiz. I didn't realize how much I enjoyed receiving and giving gifts to others just as much as spending quality time with my family. And because hospitality was a natural gift of mine, Acts of Service fit right into my love of giving. Acts of Service are when others feel loved when you do a specific activity for them, whether they ask for this support or not.

Understanding my love language helped me develop my true character in how I think, feel, and behave when giving or showing love. I highly encourage you to take the "Love Language Quiz" to discover your natural gifts in expressing your love to others around you. Once you have defined your love languages, you can implement those gifts into finding your calling in life.

THE FIRST FRUIT

Being a housewife, I enjoyed hosting and showing great hospitality to any guests who visited. It is a service I enjoy doing the most at no cost. Displaying this love language for me is a physical service, showing others that I am willing to do the work versus talking about it. Seeing and feeling others embracing my warmth and generosity, along with being appreciative of my service, meant a lot to me. Living my life solely as a housewife was very delightful.

I truly enjoyed cooking, hosting, and spending time with family and friends. However, having that title alone only made me question if there was more to life than doing the work inside the walls of my home. It made me self-reflect if my calling was more than just my family's needs. As my children grew to an age where they became self-sufficient and didn't need me as much, I knew it was time for a change. At the time, my husband worked at a successful automotive dealership as General Manager, managing multiple dealerships in the area. Since my kids and husband didn't need much attention, I knew my time at home daily was not a high obligation. I had now hit the milestone of being a daily housewife of those ritual routines. I knew I was ready to live a life where I could be creative and passionate about doing something more than being a mom or wife. I was ready to desire something more extensive than what my home walls could hold.

As I started to take that courageous leap of faith by walking into establishing something new in my life, I began to feel a sense of fear creeping in. It was fear of the unknown, not knowing what to expect. I became fearful of failing. Even though it is a natural feeling, I was still a little scared to embrace change. Fear can sometimes stem from the possibility that situations may or may not work in your favor. Being frightened is to be afraid to live a bountiful life. No one knows what the future will hold, but if you have hope for the future, then that's one step away from being fearful and afraid.

If you want to live out your purpose, you must be willing to take chances and do what your heart is compelling. Things you have been dreaming of doing but now are too afraid of potential failure or making mistakes. Most people are only comfortable achieving things they are good at doing. However, just because you are good and comfortable at doing something does not mean you are living for your purpose. I had to remind myself of this quote, "Life begins at the end of your comfort zone"[5]. Thinking about how true this quote is made me think more about my life and potential outside the housewife title.

My years as a sole housewife brought comfort and ease to my daily life. I was very comfortable with my life, and there wasn't much-uninterrupted occurrence happening in my household that made me challenge myself. Therefore, I became bored, lacking interest in who I was. I was too wrapped up in my comfort zone of living a day-to-day home lifestyle. I lived in a psychological state where most people felt at ease because of the lack of being challenged. In this comfort zone, people don't typically engage in new experiences or take on challenges. They only participate in routine activities, making them feel "in control" of their environment.

That was me.

I was living in that stage where everything was going well, and no turmoil was brewing. Life was good. My life was good as a homemaker, but my mission meant more. I knew I had more energy inside me that was ready to be burned. I knew there

---

[5] Inspirational Quote from Neale Donald Walsch

were valuable opportunities with resources and knowledge with my name on them. I wasn't looking for a particular hobby or activity to keep me busy while my kids and husband were away. But I was looking for something a little more fulfilling.

The type of fulfillment I was looking for was more than just your typical work. I wasn't bored because I needed something to do or wanted to pass the time. But instead, I had a spark that needed to be lighted, a deep desire to walk into my purpose. Sometimes when you feel bored, it doesn't mean it's time to get a hobby. It means you are not living your entire purpose and calling in life. You will know because your daily work will become tedious, involving mental or physical effort to achieve a given task. But note that this type of work is basic and nothing more. This typical basic work can bring challenges, mishaps, disappointments, and the determination to keep trying repeatedly.

In most cases, if not all, basic work is necessary for any job-related field and is essential in everyday life. However, the work I sought had a more significant meaning than just getting a job done.

When you realize that your life is worth more than what is being perceived, you will want to live a motivated life full of reasoning. To live on purpose means to live a life with meaning and substance. A person full of purpose adds value to the world. Their merits are of good worth, and they will continue to live for a long time. Living a purposeful life is moving towards a big goal that aligns with your values and passions and makes you happy. **The real purpose in life is to love what you do and do what you love.** If you never get paid for doing what you love, will you be okay with that? If you said yes, you are living a life full of good deeds that will bring everlasting joy and contentment. Your skills, talent, and knowing your love language will be essential when discovering your life purpose. Once you discover it, you can genuinely pour your heart into doing something gratifying and fulfilling. The next step will be determining what type of work (your calling) you will do.

In deciding my next step from housewife to a notable career, I knew I had a burning passion for teaching, educating, and growing others in their learning. My love for education stemmed from a very early age in my life. As a child, I loved playing with my stuffed animals and pretending to be their teacher. I would pretend to teach them life lessons and how to solve numerous math problems. There were also times when I would pretend to take them to the nurse's office if they were hurt or in severe pain. Back then, I had an imaginable, make-believe mind that one could only dream of as a kid. In those moments of pretending in my make-believe world, I enjoyed the concept of being a teacher and nurse. The love I had encountered at an early age for this profession made me want to pursue it even more once I came of age. With that same gleam of passion, I began pursuing my career as a teacher.

In pursuing my career as a teacher, my first thought was about something other than the money I would make. I knew I was entering a profession where the pay scale was at the bottom of the pole. If you are not aware, let me be the first to inform you that teachers make less money compared to other occupations. It is one of the lowest-paid professional fields to enter the workforce. However, teachers will make the most significant impact on the lives of many students. My purpose of becoming a teacher had a greater mission than receiving a paycheck. I wanted to love what I did as a child and continue that love as an adult.

When you are passionate about doing something that brings love and joy, you will want to pursue it. Pursuing this love of becoming a teacher to educate and grow others was a life commitment that, at the time, I didn't know would be a part of my purpose and calling. I finally started to understand the true meaning of living a purposeful life: and that was to give love to your life.

Note to Self-Reflect:

If you want to gain love, it's time to start living for your purpose. Whether you are a mom, wife, sister, or daughter, think of the things you once dreamed of pursuing before you started carrying your current title. Next, write down what it is that sparked your interest and how those things inspired you as a person. Then, once you have rekindled your true passion for what you want to do, write down your reasoning for wanting to pursue it. As you begin to write, you will notice a joy of excitement leaping from your soul that will awaken your natural gifts. Your natural gifts are the talent and skills deeply bestowed on you. It's the gifts you have been born with since you were in your mother's womb. It can sometimes be challenging for most people to discover their true gifts in life. But all you need is a piece of paper to start listing your strengths, skills, and abilities. This minor assignment will be the first initiative to discover or redefine your purpose in life.

While discovering your natural talent and gifts, there will be moments when you may begin to second-guess your purpose in life. Remember, feeling scared or afraid when embracing change or starting something new is a natural feeling. Surround yourself with people who will motivate, support, and reassure you that what you are doing or about to do in life is beneficial. When you have genuine compassion for living life on purpose, then nothing will be able to hinder you from seeking out your true calling. Once you realize what brings you joy, you will want to do more of it but on a bigger scale.

Again, if you never make one dollar fulfilling your purpose, will you be okay with it? Remember not to let money, fame, titles, or power define your true purpose in life. Those things are significant benefits to reap if your heart is in the right place and with the right people. And eventually, those benefits will come naturally without you trying to aim for them. Remember,

THE FIRST FRUIT

your purpose is a special calling that only you can fulfill based on the gifts God has given you. Try to avoid second-guessing your calling. Instead of having doubts about what you should be doing in life, have a conversation with God. Ask HIM for wisdom, knowledge, and understanding of what HE has planned for you. Sometimes the answer you seek is a simple awareness that stares at you all day. Begin to keep a journal of your day's reflection and think about how you can change a given situation if you have the opportunity to. Self-reflection is an excellent key factor in how you want to live out your life and how you want to impact others positively.

When you are self-aware of what you love to do, you will live life more freely. Your days will bring laughter and happiness in situations that may seem unenjoyable. You will begin to walk confidently, knowing your life has a purpose. The gifts and talents you now have will impact the hearts and minds of many people. So, now that you discovered what you love to do most in life, take a moment to embrace it.

Now is a time of joy and celebration because you understand the importance of walking in your purpose.

Joy

The Second Fruit

Chapter 2:

No Plan. No Worries. There's still JOY.

"A goal without a Plan is just a wish." –Unknown

It was like yesterday, my first day as a certified, qualified teacher in a public school. What a joy it was to know I was moving along a direction of life that I envisioned for myself. Before working in the public-school sector, I worked at my local church as a children's Sunday school teacher, teaching ages 3-5 years old. I also assisted in youth ministry and helped establish a Mother's Day Out program. It wasn't just my level of volunteer work, but I wanted to give back to the community and show my love for Christ by teaching HIS word. It is always a joyful moment to do something that brings happiness and zeal to your life. Have you ever volunteered (without a paycheck) and enjoyed it so much that you wanted to do it more? Doing something for others can be very gratifying in your life. It's a satisfactory feeling that will not feel forced, but instead, it will feel rewarding. Your purpose will never be something forced upon you. It will come naturally, and your deeds will be shown as authentic and genuine.

As I continued volunteering in my community, I wanted to pursue my dream of becoming a teacher even more. Being a stay-at-home housewife for six years, I have worked deliberately in the children's ministry at my local church and participated in other charitable events in the area. With minimal accreditation added to my resume, my credentials as a Bible school teacher, along with facilitating a Mother's Day Out program, eventually qualified me as an advocate for child development and a candidate for a teacher leadership role. Therefore, I achieved a Bachelor of Arts in Family and Child Studies with a minor in Psychology. I also received an Alternative Degree in Education, which led me to earn a pedagogy and teacher certification.

Having these degrees and certificates added to my resume made me feel more qualified and ready to be the best teacher I could be. At least, that's what I believed at that time.

THE SECOND FRUIT

When my first big day approached, it was a day I will never forget. September 10, 2010. It was a Friday, the last day of the week. I was hired in July of that same year, but the school district I was set to work at took forever to process all the paperwork. The anticipation of waiting can be draining when you are a new teacher excited to embrace the new journey. I was hired as a 2nd-grade self-contained teacher.

Being new to the industry, I didn't know what self-contained meant or had any prior knowledge about the public schools' lingo. The only thing wandering in my mind was that I was about to start a career, a journey, outside of being a housewife. So when I received the call from the principal saying I had the job, I didn't ask any questions about the position; I just responded with, "Yes, I'll take it!". At that moment, I knew my life was about to change. So accepting this offer was more than just taking a position. But instead, it was a commitment that I was willing to embrace.

When your dream becomes a reality, it's time for a call to action. A *dream* written down with a date becomes a *goal*. A goal broken down into steps becomes a *plan*. A plan backed by

JOY

action makes your dreams a *reality*[6]. If you are not dreaming of accomplishing something in life, then you are not living life to its fullest. To have no goals or aspirations is to live a droughtful life.

I was ecstatic to have the opportunity to be someone whom I imagined as a little girl. Even though I had taught Sunday school children's ministry, accepting a teaching position in a public-school setting was a dream of mine because I now had the opportunity to reach more kids.

As I waited and waited and waited for the district to call to sign my contract, I continued living my daily routine as a mom, wife, and homemaker.

The anticipation of waiting grew stronger and stronger as the days passed, eventually leading to weeks. All I could hear was my mom saying, "Be patient; they will call you." Finally, after a month passed and still no word on signing my contract, I became anxious. I started questioning whether teaching in a public school was my right calling. I was beginning to lose the joy I had first encountered when I received that phone call. My excitement was dwindling, and despair was creeping into my mind.

---

[6] Inspirational Quote by Unknown

I have been mentally and physically preparing myself to be a teacher this whole time. It has been on my list of goals I wanted to accomplish. I had done the logistics of attending college to study its functionality and received my teacher certifications. I had done everything on my part that I could have done to help me get to this point. Now I just had to keep waiting and trusting God the school district would call soon to sign my contract and make it official.

Have you been in a situation where things were going as planned, but then you found yourself in a stand-still state? God will put you in circumstances where your patience, faith, and calling will be tested. When you find yourself in this predicament, praise God for what is about to happen.

While waiting, I decided to use this time to be productive and start making cute decorations for my classroom. I wanted to make learning fun and engaging. One of the fun parts of becoming a teacher is exercising the creative and innovative skills that most teachers have. Although being creative had its pleasurable moment, thinking back on the situation, making those crafty decorations probably should not have been my top priority. But in despair of waiting, I needed something to

JOY

bring my joy back. I was simultaneously losing my excitement and the focus of my purpose of being a teacher. Instead of making arts and crafts, I should have been researching the school's demographic and reading about the school's Campus Improvement Plan (CIP). I should have been preparing my mind and planning how I would capture the heart and minds of my students.

In situations like this one, where there is little hope of joy that is slowly being lost, most people start to find themselves distracted by other things that are not as important. If you are one of those people faced with a deafening silence of waiting, this is the time to prepare yourself for the focus point of your purpose. Focusing on the important areas will be pivotal in helping you accomplish your goals. There will be circumstances when some things will seem unjustifiably on why certain situations have occurred or have been prolonged for an extensive amount of time. When that happens, don't let your mind wander to a place of second-guessing. Every waiting period has an undefinable expiration date. You just have to be willing to wait and trust the process.

After three months of waiting, the district finally called me to sign my contract (hallelujah). It was

THE SECOND FRUIT

Thursday, September 9, 2010, noon. Still, today I'm not sure why they took so long to call me, but I was exhilarated to get the call. As a witness of this immeasurable waiting period, if you are waiting for something to happen, I strongly encourage you to stay positive and trust it will come to pass, even if it takes a long time. Until you get the news, then no news is good news.

I was so excited and thrilled once I received the news, I rushed to the district office before they would have changed their mind. As soon as I signed, I went to my new campus to let the principal know I was ready to start. She took me around the campus for the first time since the building was being remodeled over the summer break. During that moment, I had the opportunity to meet all my coworkers, including the Assistant Principal, and see where my classroom would be for the first time. I didn't get to meet my students because the class was already in session, and we didn't want to interrupt the learning. So many staff members welcomed me with warmth, smiles, and hugs. I was so joyous to be in an environment where I felt accepted.

After showing me around the building, my principal congratulated me again on the new position and told me to report to work the next

JOY

day at 8 am. I politely looked at her in her eyes with excitement and said, "Yes, ma'am, will do." This housewife was ready to embrace her new journey as a teacher. I went home and put together a cute outfit because we all know you feel empowered when you look your best. My husband and kids were super excited for me. I was so pumped to know my family was so supportive. I planned to go to bed early and get a good night's rest so I could be ready to start setting up my new classroom with all those cute decorations I had made while waiting to hear from the district.

Because I had started three weeks into the school year, I didn't have time to set up my classroom and greet parents and students for "meet the teacher day" or even plan with my colleagues what I was supposed to be teaching. Also, since my position was classified as a self-contained teacher, I had to make lesson plans to teach all these credible subjects. For a self-contained teacher teaching second grade, these subjects consisted of math, science, social studies, reading, writing, spelling, and social skills. Yes, even social skills. And there were no written scripts provided by the school district or any curriculum for new teachers to abide by at that time. The only thing provided was the state's essential knowledge and skills performance

THE SECOND FRUIT

standards. These standards were the foundation of what I was required to teach; as far as the lesson, I had to be creative in my delivery.

It was my BIG day. I arrived at my new job early on Friday morning. Everyone greeted me with warmth again; my principal showed me my classroom and said, "Have a good day." I was excited until the bell rang, and the students were released to enter the school. Then I realized I didn't have a plan. I didn't know what I was supposed to do with the students. I didn't have a schedule or a lesson plan to guide me through the day. All the other teachers were occupied with their students in their classrooms. At that moment, I was feeling out of place. I just wanted to cry. My skills in teaching Sunday school and children's ministry were nowhere near what I faced. I had 18 seven-year-old students looking at me, waiting for me to teach them. I didn't know what to do. I tried as much to wing it as possible. I was drowning and scared I would not make it through the day. Just as I was about to wave the white flag of surrender, a teacher named Mrs. Pearson came in to help me. I was so grateful for her help. She later became my mentor.

God always knows when to send help at the right time. The Bible states that "God will never

JOY

leave you or forsake you. So do not be afraid or discouraged"[7]. Looking into my student's eyes at that moment gave me the ambition to keep being their teacher. After being without a teacher for three weeks, they needed someone who wouldn't leave them. And I needed to show them that I was the right teacher. Thank goodness they were friendly, pleasant, and gentle to me. They showed me what to do and where to find things around the classroom. They even showed me where the schedule was, which was in plain sight on the whiteboard.

As soon as I got home, I started planning right away. I didn't; allow anything to distract me from being ready on Monday. I was so thankful for the weekend; it gave me time to create a plan. The funny part about this story is I received the job offer in July and officially started in September. Given two months to prep and strategies, you would think I would've been well-ready & equipped for the 1st day. But, sometimes, it only takes one moment to know you never want to be in a situation or position where you feel helpless, unprepared, and dumbfounded. I was so caught up in getting the job that I didn't allow myself to

---

[7] Scripture from Deuteronomy 31:8

process what would happen next. I was still stuck in the moment of hearing, "you got the position."

In chapter 4, I will talk more about "NOT" staying too stuck in an area of enthusiasm.

Remember that a goal without a plan is just another wish. Don't get caught up wishing for greatness; start planning how you will achieve it.

Note to Self-Reflect:

There will be moments in your life when you will get so excited about the future and even thrilled about its passing. But then fail to put a plan into action. Unfortunately, situations like this will occur more often than intended. When you find yourself in this situation, this is the time to put forth your faith even more. This is when you will want to start to believe and pray for something that you know can happen for good.

I want you to think of a time when you prayed for something that didn't turn out as you intended. How did it make you feel? Did you want to give up since things were not working in your favor? Sometimes having those rollercoaster emotions can test a person's faith.

JOY

But on the contrary, being in that long waiting period can also give you the required time needed to help prepare you for a successful walk of life. Remember, a *dream* backed up by a *goal* with steps of a *plan* will eventually become a *reality*.

Sometimes when waiting for a call or final decision, you have to be productive with that time. That time is for you to cultivate the soil before planting the seeds. Instead of getting caught up in worrying thoughts, let your excitement overflow into your planning stage. Use that allotted wait time to brainstorm how you will overcome obstacles you may encounter. Make notes of questions or ideas you want to implement once you start your first big day.

Be cautious not to let anxiety get you so eager to the point where you forget to put a plan in place.

Create a roadmap, from start to finish, on how you want to envision living your life. Make sure to add a few roadblocks or detour signs because living in your purpose can get bumpy. Being overzealous about how your destination will look can sometimes send a person in a thrill of high hopes. Unfortunately, those high hopes can sometimes become disappointments if you cannot endure the whole mission of your calling. When not fit to run, most people run a race (answer a calling) when they are not ready to run. So how do you know if you are prepared to run your next race (calling)? To help you answer that question, write down what credentials you have stored up that will make you qualified for your next race (mission).

Once you have made a list of your accredited accomplishments or high skill sets, make another list of supporters that will help you stay focused on your purpose. My mom, sister, and husband always reminded me to see the glass half-full versus half-empty. This metaphor symbolizes that there will be other opportunities to gain from. And if a particular plan does not work in my favor or my timing, don't worry.

Think of a time when you had an opportunity that was presented but then got delayed. How did it set back your original plans? Were there other focus points to keep the joy of your goals going? Better yet, what about any distractions that kept you from focusing? Was there anything that distracted you from continuing your plan of action? These are all self-reflection questions to consider if you are in an undesirable situation.

In life, there will be distractions that you will face, and they will derail you from being optimistic, causing discontent and constant worrying. I'm here to tell you not to let distractions distract you from focusing on what you are supposed to be doing with your life, purpose, and calling. Distraction is the key factor that gets you sidetracked from things with no actual value. For example, too much social media can be a huge distraction. Getting caught up in the social media world of seeing what other people are doing can have little to no effect on what you are trying to accomplish or gain. Those social elite media distractions can cause you to live a false lifestyle that will not be an authentic version of who you are. Don't be one of those people who are so busy trying to live or run in someone else's lane that now you can't focus on what God is calling you to do. I'm here to tell you if you don't separate yourself from your distractions, your distractions will separate you from your goal and the life you want. The best way to stay focused is by always preparing and planning to reach your next set of goals. By being productive, proactive, and purposeful, create your plan of what you were meant to do. And be passionate about what you are willing to give.

If you're having uncertainties about going about your calling, here are some pointers to help guide you: 1. React with excitement knowing you

THE SECOND FRUIT

can make a difference in the world. 2. Let your enthusiasm lead you to want to know more about the position you're about to take on. 3. Make the initiative to call your support team (family members, friends, and loved ones) to let them know you are going to be embracing this new journey. You will need their prayers and support. 4. Ask your new employer or colleague if it's okay to contact other team members and get connected immediately! Your calling is too crucial for you not to enjoy the process.

Based on my experience, I advise you not to wait too long to connect with your new team members as I did. If given an opportunity, be an initiator and introduce yourself and your skill strengths to your new team. When given a chance, you will never know how much of a first impression you can have on a person's life. On the contrary, you will never know how much a person can assist you while in that waiting stage of your new career. Remember that not everyone will experience the same level of journey entry as you may. Therefore, it is essential to note where you are in the preparation stage of encountering your new career. Most importantly, let it be known to your leader, or if you are the leader, how serious you are willing to invest in your new position. When investing in something, you are showing your effort, commitment, extra time, or resources you are eager to give to make sure what you are about to do will be spectacular. It is also essential to educate yourself on the responsibilities of your new position. You can do that by looking up the entity's mission statement, the demographics of your clientele, the content/subject areas that you will be working with, the requirements of the job duties, or even reading books that correlate with the job descriptions. These are great tips that will prepare you for what's next to come.

If your next journey is going into the profession of education, then I highly recommend you read Harry Wong, *The First Days of School; How to Be an Effective Teacher*. It's a book guided with helpful tips on how to be an effective teacher during your first days of school. He quotes, "*We teach you to plan so you can plan to teach*". The book elaborates on how to plan and what resources and tools to use while planning, and it describes the different methods you can use to hook students' engagement. This book is just one of the many other great reads to help you if your next journey is in education.

Whatever your next direction in life is, there will be plenty of resources out there that can help you get ready. You must be willing to put in the effort and take action. Living in the 21st century, you now have access to online resources just a few clicks away. You can only claim ignorance if you don't allow your mind to be open. Your mind will give back exactly what you put into it. The knowledge you will gain from these resources will be essential to your journey. Start implementing positive thoughts in your mind knowing you are meant to serve this purpose and that you are the right person for the job. Store up as much information in your mind, and when the time comes, you will be equipped to use it. You will have all the tools in your toolbox ready to handle any mishaps that may come your way. Because of your commitment to preparing and planning, you now will have the confidence you need and won't be afraid to fail.

To have true joy in life is to know you will live a life of possibilities that eventually turn into realities. Even when you may not have a specific plan to navigate those unforeseen challenges, there will be no need to worry because God will give you the peace needed to continue your journey.

Peace

The Third Fruit

Chapter 3

The Visit. PEACE be unto you.

"Every single thing that has ever happened in your life is preparing you for a moment that is yet to come"
—*Unknown*

Everyone wants to visit when you are the new teacher on the block to see how things are going. There is the principal, the assistant principal, the instructional coaches, the mentor, the counselor, and then the grade-level team leader. When you think you have the perfect plan, here comes everyone's input. My classroom management feedback was mostly positive, with a few constructive criticisms on the teaching part. I was open-minded about getting as much feedback as possible whenever it was given to me. Because teaching was new to me, I had to learn many acronyms, what they meant, and when to use them correctly.

I swiftly learned the many components when it came to teaching. Did you know teachers are responsible for designing the lesson, selecting content, understanding the different delivery styles, assessing, and reflecting on the student's learning ability? Their ongoing engagement with the student is imperative to enable the student's understanding and application of knowledge, concepts, and processes. Because reading is fundamental in a child's primary stage, assessing the student's reading ability is vital. At the time, I didn't realize the importance of pre-assessing students. As educators, you should get to know your students on all levels: personal and academic. It does require a lot of prep work, late-night readings, weekend conferences, parent phone calls, and other necessities. When you are eager for change and success, your mind will not be programmed to a 9-5 work shift.

After many visits from the counselor, the resource teacher, the speech pathologist, the behavior specialist, and the diagnostician lady, I realized this was a peculiar class. In this class, different characteristic behaviors must be accommodated based on each student's unusual awareness. And yes, I was right. I had all the behaviors, low achievers,

THE THIRD FRUIT

retainers, barrier languages, English Language Learners (ELLs), and Special Education (SpEd) students. I asked myself, why would they give the new teacher, with no experience, all these kids with all these special needs and accommodations?

Being new with no experience on this level, I knew the challenge of learning these different needs would have been immense. I would need a concept or guided map on how to teach them at their level and pace. At first, I told myself that this was a joke or even a secret plan to make me quit because I was new to this environment.

Proverbs 16:9 (NLT) states, "We can make our plan, but the Lord determines our steps." Just know when God has a plan for you, HE never makes mistakes. God put me right where I needed to be in a position to humble and educate myself on my students' awareness. I didn't know at the time that this class of students was a part of my purpose.

Knowing your purpose in life will make you more susceptible to understanding your calling. After all, I was still excited to be a teacher; I' just didn't know how to be one on this level. I quickly became fearful of learning how to teach different personalities and learning traits. When I envisioned myself as a teacher, I only pictured the perfect class with no learning disabilities and only positive outcomes. The type of outcome of seeing students enjoying their learning while in a safe environment. I never imagined there was more to the work of a teacher or what was being perceived. When I look at the life of a teacher, I see them teaching the lesson, making connections with their students, and celebrating their achievements. It didn't dawn on me that every student will not have the same learning abilities. At that moment, I knew I had to prevail as a teacher and an individual who was truly ready to walk in my calling.

Within my first year, I attended as many professional developments (PD) classes, courses, and sessions as I could be a part of that year. My students needed me, and I needed to be ready to get them to the next level. I read numerous books and collaborated with other campus and district teachers with students with similar needs. I had many students from various backgrounds, culturally speaking, with language barriers which made learning difficult to achieve. I had to equip myself to learn how to plan lessons and teach with diversity in mind. There was no cookie-cutter style of teaching when it came to my students. I had to educate myself on how to be proactive and proficient for the well-being of my student's academic learning.

Therefore, I went to take the English as Second Language (ESL) exam to be certified in that area. I wasn't bilingual, but I had to think and design my lessons as if I was teaching a dual language class. I joined the Language Proficiency Assessment Committee (LPAC), which allowed me to work with students with multiple languages and set standards to help them learn. I sat in Annual Review & Dismissal (ARDs) meetings, reviewed Individual Evaluation Plans (IEP), and joined the Response to Intervention (RtI) committee, which helped me understand students' pace of learning and what accommodations and modifications to give them so they too can be just as successful as their peers.

I participated in the Site Based Decision Making (SBDM) committee and later became the Gifted and Talented (GT) committee chairperson. Working with GT students challenged me to elevate myself to think outside the box on a higher level of critical thinking, where I could've pushed them to a place where rigorous and relevant learning can occur.

I did whatever was necessary for my students to WIN. The word W.I.N. is an acronym that my colleagues and I later came up with to help serve our small group tutorial sessions. It stands for *Whatever Is Necessary*. It was the motto I had in mind when it came to the learning habits of my students.

My principal was thrilled with the idea and eventually made it a whole campus initiative starting from grade levels pre-k to fifth grade. This initiative aimed to help close the gaps in academic achievement. The inspiration of these W.I.N. groups focused on the student's learning deficiency which kept them from grasping the learning objective of what was being taught. These small groups would take place daily for thirty-minute all at the same time. Therefore, no student would be left behind in learning new concepts. This enthusiasm for learning was the level of empathy my colleagues and I were passionate about regarding the success of students' learning modalities. As a determined teacher, I wanted my students' parents to know we had a plan for their child's academic success. I also wanted to validate with my principal that she made the right decision in hiring me.

Being a part of those committees brought a different learning awareness that I was unaware of initially. It also motivated me to advocate for learning diversity for all children and students of all disabilities from racially, ethnically, culturally, and linguistically diverse communities and backgrounds. These committees gave me the knowledge I needed to be humble in the gifts that God has given me. Without this type of support, I would not have been as successful in implementing the necessary accommodations and modifications that my students needed.

With the proper support and resources, I was ready to soak up as much information as possible. I was willing to visit other campuses and teachers' classrooms who taught a different subject than me to see the strategies they would use to help close the academic learning gaps. Learning from different teaching methods like student-centered discussions, making connections, increasing autonomy, and building relationships focused on literacy enabled me and my lessons to be more cohesive with the student's learning. Also, learning different approaches to engage, explore, explain, elaborate, and evaluate a student's learning behavior was vital for the growth of any teacher. Having those opportunities to watch and learn from a similar peer shows a level of development in which one is willing to create change and progress for a more significant cause. In my observation learning stages, I have been very gracious to work with coworkers willing to share their skills and methods so I can keep teaching with fidelity.

As an educator with various opportunities to learn from other educators, it is imperative to surround yourself with people who are like-minded as yourself. Their positivity and determination for student achievement help boost morale not just for me but for the greater good of the whole community. When supporting another person in their achievement, the level of support can be more rewarding to you than the other person. When you see greatness and potential in others, be a cheerleader and encourage them on their journey. Be the biggest cheerleader anyone can ask for, always rooting for another to win and succeed. When you show that you can support another person's growth, that person will want to continue to do their best at what they love to do. When you are a part of something other than yourself, you'll feel motivated to see others achieve greatness.

In 2001, former president George W. Bush passed an act called No Child Left Behind. It was signed into law on January 8, 2002; the purpose of the "act" is to ensure that students in every public school achieve essential learning goals while being educated in safe classrooms by well-prepared teachers. In other words, no child (student) would fail or be pushed into a corner because they couldn't keep up with their peers academically. In reinforcing this act, it is up to the teacher to go the extra mile and help students attain a healthy learning habit that will be enjoyable for their learning growth spurt. Until the student is self-sufficient in their learning, it is the teacher's responsibility, along with the support of the parents, to make sure no student is left lacking in their ability to learn.

In some professions, like a teacher, this "act" symbolizes the importance of the mission of a teacher.

For me, as a teacher, understanding my purpose and knowing my calling in life impacted the decisions I made as an educator. My actions, which included going the extra mile and taking additional steps, were necessary to reflect the goals I had put in place not just as an individual but as a leader willing to make a difference in a student's life. Even though I had to revise my plans due to unaware circumstances, like not knowing that all students do not learn at the same rate, it made me more cognitive on how I would go about assessing the situations. Because of the multiple people coming to my classroom daily, I began asking questions about why all the frequent visits. Once I was aware of my position, it was up to me to decide if I would quit or endure. With no previous accolades from this teaching experience, I could have allowed myself to go into a place of panic or peace, knowing God would give me all the necessary resources to fulfill this calling. Because of my obedience to answer my call as a teacher, I became emotional to learn and grow about my student's learning disabilities. My students were only a part of my journey for a season. And in that season, it was my responsibility, as their teacher, to plant seeds that would close the missing learning gaps.

This scenario made me learn you should never be too complacent in your life, career, or position where you are not willing to be compassionate for others. The things you are passionate about will never be random because they will be a part of your calling and purpose. Knowing your purpose, answering your calling, and aligning it with what you do daily will change your life forever.

Remember that everything that has ever happened to you at this point in life prepares you for a moment yet to come.

Note to Self-Reflect:

You will have moments when God pushes you to see if you are doing what you're supposed to be doing with your calling and gifts. That test will come in various forms, like unexpected people showing up in your life when you least expect it. Or even having numerous people come in and out of your life to bring you the same message but in a different delivery. When those moments happen, be cognitive of the nature of those visits. Don't be quick to brush those types of visitors off or think it was just a coincidence they stopped by. God always has a unique way of getting your attention. And HE will use other people as a vessel to get to you, to see the bigger picture, the more significant cause, so you can go about and make changes. HE will also put you in unique situations to know if you have the assurance to keep going.

When you find yourself being tested, the first thing is to recognize it is a test. Remember not to let yourself get in a fragile state of mind thinking someone is playing a joke on you. Better yet, don't start thinking you cannot sustain whatever difficult situation will hit you. When you attest to a particular calling in your life, note you will only get the headline of the assignment. God will not give you the specifics or details of every encounter you will face while living out your calling. HE wants you to trust HIM and know you can do the assignment. There is a reason why HE specifically called "you" to carry out this assignment. Sometimes, you may never know or be able to grasp the concept. Only HE knows what trials and tribulations you are capable of handling. And HE will give you the willpower to pass the test if you apply HIS peace to get you through.

Not all situations you will encounter will be predicted or planned. But instead, you will have to discern which ones are unexpected. There will be a warning sign for you to adhere to when that time comes.

THE THIRD FRUIT

Ask God for wisdom to be alerted to hear and see the signs. Let's take a moment to self-reflect. Think of a time when you encountered a situation where you knew something didn't seem or feel right. Do you have a time in mind? After too many ongoing visitors coming into my classrooms, I realized something was wrong. At the time, being a new teacher, I had assumed the constant visitations were for me. And in those moments of not knowing better, I didn't realize the visits weren't for me, but it was to check how the students were learning. However, I was still appreciative of thinking those visits were to check on me, ensuring I was in good standards with protocols and procedures. I had yet to inform myself that I had a class where many accommodations and modifications needed to be in place. I probably would not have accepted the position if someone had told me about the many learning deficiencies I would have faced. But because of my joy and excitement to walk into my calling, I had to humble myself. First, being thankful for the opportunity to teach. And second, for the chance to learn more about my students' learning needs.

In most cases, you, too, will find yourself in situations where you are faced with information that will help you plan for a more effective calling.

Remember that some things will come unexpectedly, throwing you into a panic state. When those unexpected moments approach you, it's up to you how you will react. There will be situations where you will not agree with every feedback, suggestion, or advice. When those situations arise, I strongly encourage you to listen before reacting. Take whatever feedback that is presented into consideration. Sometimes it can be challenging to see something from a distance, even if you are up close to it. All feedback does not mean you are doing something wrong. It may be the information you need to get better. It can be information to help improve your skills and techniques. Being reciprocal to feedback shows you are capable of growing. It shows that you are a person who is open-minded, attentive to listening, and proactive for change. When you are willing to accept feedback and learn from it, you will want to invest more time and effort into the task given to you.

Your invested time that you will put into learning more about how to help others achieve greatness will come back to you in abundance overflowing with good fruits. You will have the ultimate decision to make a difference in the lives of the people around you. The decision you choose can bring life or death into someone's being. You can choose to be a vibrant person, full of energy and enthusiasm, or a vapid person who offers nothing stimulating and challenging. You can choose to be a welcoming person or an unwelcoming person. A person who seeks answers to the problem or doesn't care about finding a solution: your reaction, response, and choice will always be yours to make. I highly recommend you be someone everyone wants to hang around, visit, or be in their company. That person brings good energy and wishes others well in their endeavors. **You will only get peace in your life when you know you're doing good in the life of others.** Nothing is more peaceful than to know you have given it your all and your all meant well.

When you have peace and comfort knowing life will produce goodness, you will be ready to receive any visitor, unexpected circumstances, and challenging tests coming your way. You will be prepared and excited to continue to plant more seeds of life soon. The work you have put in leading to this point in your life will not be in vain. Because of your dedication, endurance, and patience, you will now see the gratification of your harvest starting to blossom.

Patience

The Fourth Fruit

Chapter 4

Have *PATIENCE*. And you will reap the benefits.

We live in a world full of fast-paced technology, where everything is just a fingertip/touch away. Instead of waiting for the mail, you can now check your email or a website to find the information you're looking for within a minute. Instead of waiting for a taxi, you can Uber or Lyft, and they'll be there in less than five minutes. Instead of waiting to find out the sex of the baby, a mother can now choose to have the sex of her baby impregnated. We, as a nation, no longer bear patience; instead, we yearn for the next great thing to come within seconds. With a fast-growing world wanting to reach and accomplish goals, sometimes we neglect to pause and enjoy important milestones.

Enjoying each small occurring moment can be more gratifying than that which leads to a grand finale. The process of waiting to see how something is going to turn out makes life worth living. In other words, having the patience to keep doing something without losing interest or becoming anxious can lead to a life full of enjoyable moments.

I read "Enjoy the Ride" by Steven Gilland in my many readings of various self-awareness books. The book is a self-reflection of one's life that talks about the actual ride or events one will go through while leading up to their destination. For example, in a school year, there are typically nine months that make up a calendar year. In those nine months, there are certain events that a teacher/student/parent will go through before the year comes to an end. In that calendar year, there's the first day of school, the beginning of the year pre-assessments, fall/winter break, mid-year assessments, spring break, and the end of the year assessments. During those big, highlighted moments are the different types of school functions and activities, extracurricular after-school programs, parental night, family fun night, science fair, literacy night, etc., which one may encounter. Even though all these events are expected to happen, as predicted in the school calendar, going through each event's process will make each moment memorable. By

THE FOURTH FRUIT

the time one has reached the end of the school year, success can be celebrated because of the endurance, actions, and steps taken to achieve a good ending. The point here is that there will be events in your life that will be predictable based on what's been circulated in the past. Knowing what is expected, you can learn to "enjoy the ride" by embracing the moments and minutes of each anticipated event.

In this same book, Gilland also talks about how success is not a thing you acquire or achieve, but the journey you take throughout your life makes you successful. I must agree with this statement. Having success in life is an outcome of how you live it. Your approach and actions on how you use the given time and moments will make you see life differently.

When I accepted my calling as a teacher, I went through a series of events that felt like I was on a roller coaster of ups and downs of emotions. There were days when I felt excited, and there were days when I didn't want to be bothered or do anything. My mom, being the woman of God that she is, would tell me, "Daughter, know that you will go through storms in your life. You will be either entering a storm, being in the midst of a storm, or coming out of a storm". She would let me know this was a part of life's journey, and it was up to me how I wanted to react to the storm that I was currently in. When I processed what she told me, I knew I had to push harder to overcome those rainy days and drive towards the goals I once set for myself. In those moments, I realized I needed to appreciate life's roller coaster of emotions and be thankful for the more incredible days to come.

Now that the ride of becoming a teacher was over, I had surpassed that moment. It was time for me to apply what I had learned through readings and experiences and now use it to my student's learning needs.

In my first-year teaching, my primary goal was not to quit and to see all my students succeed in 3rd grade, which eventually they did. The first year of starting anything new in life can be challenging. Because I was so determined to be successful at seeing the growth and well-being of my student's learning, I encountered many late nights of studying different learning patterns, understanding cultural diversity, and making modifications to accommodate the different behavior styles. To be relevant and reachable to my students, I had to do a deep, extensive study to learn and understand who they were. I had to learn eighteen different personalities and what will motivate them to learn effectively. This level of responsibility for me was more than just a job and receiving a paycheck. But instead, it was important to me to go the extra mile. At this point, I was too deep into my calling without turning back. I was all in as their teacher.

As mentioned before, teachers' pay grade/salary is not at the top of the market for making money. It's more about impacting students' lives and changing the trajectory of how one learns than receiving a paycheck. The meaning of being a teacher goes more profound than its title. And not every person is called for this type of ministry. Yes, teaching is a type of ministry, believe it or not. You must be rooted in this ministry to withstand all weathering regarding this type of call to action. If becoming a teacher/educator is a part of your calling in life, then make sure you are going in with a true purpose. The biggest paycheck as a teacher will be making a difference in students' lives, academically and personally. No dollar amount can equal the price you will give to a student's education. For me, receiving any type of award or recognition for a ministry that brought me such joy was something I would never imagine.

As a green teacher (not fully experienced yet), I was unaware of the rewards, stipends, and accolades that most educators could receive throughout their years of teaching. In some school districts, a testing grade teacher would receive a bonus if they had high attainable state test scores. While in other school districts, some teachers would receive certain stipends based on the skills they can offer to the school or district. For example, if you speak bilingual, you are awarded a stipend. Being new with no special skills to offer but just a teacher certification was all I had at the beginning. Therefore, I was not qualified to receive a stipend or any bonuses. I didn't expect to receive more than what my pay plan was set for. And because I was just entering my career as a teacher, I never thought about getting rewarded for the work I was going to do.

In most cases, people who receive some acknowledgment, whether it's a stipend or award/reward for their work, tend to set new goals and aspirations for their future. Sometimes it is the small gratitude of receiving an incentive that can be a reminder that your work is a blessing to others and is worthy of attention. It symbolizes the tiny seeds you have been planting into the lives of others. And now those seeds have sprouted into

THE FOURTH FRUIT

good fruits worthy of special acknowledgment. Those types of acknowledgment will begin to open the minds of others to think big, expand more, and go beyond the walls of their workspace. Once I started seeing the growth and success of my student's learning patterns, I was more compelled to push myself as a teacher to set new goals for them and myself. Those new goals and aspirations eventually led me to receive several honorable awards and recognitions.

I was awarded Rookie Teacher of the Year by the end of my first year. I was humbled yet surprised that this title even existed. I've heard of the title "Teacher of the Year," but not Rookie Teacher. Really? There was an award for someone new to an organization with little experience. Again, I was very shocked but honored to receive the award. At that moment, I didn't think I deserved it. That year, we had a few new teachers at the campus, and I'm sure they were doing just as good of a job as I was. At least, that was my assumption. When you are all in, working diligently to accomplish a given goal, you won't have time to compare yourself with others in the same industry. Your focus and mentality should always be top priorities when fulfilling a calling. This inspirational quote states, "Flowers don't compete or compare with other flowers; they just blossom to share what's sweet"[8]. I believe that is a true statement regarding life and your purpose and calling. I also think every person has some sweetness to give, and that's the gift of knowledge, empowerment, encouragement, and an inspiring growth mindset. Those attributes are more rewarding than any plaque, certificate, or acknowledgment that one can receive.

After teaching second-grade self-contained for two years, my principal decided it was best to place me in 3rd grade with a focus on math and science. I went from self-contained to being departmentalized, which means dividing the subjects into sections. I was honored and excited because I could now move up with my students. But I also was a little fearful knowing I would be entering a testing grade...yikes! Teaching a testing grade brought anxiety and pressure to produce excellent test scores. Most primary grade-level teachers did not want to take on that responsibility. Therefore, there weren't many teachers who tried to move grade levels. As a teacher, you must have patience and a specific

---

[8] Inspiration Quote by Zen Shin

skill set to teach a testing grade. Now that I was moving from primary to intermediate grade, my goals had to be revised. I had to reframe my mind to think and teach differently. Changing grade levels meant meeting new team members and learning a new curriculum.

Most importantly, a new mindset. But with changes, there are always new opportunities as well.

Chances, risks, and new opportunities can all sound frightening at first. It is a normal part of life experiences that everyone will go through. But to take those chances or risks of not knowing what to expect can also bring new and exciting opportunities that one probably would only experience if one were fearless in making a move. Let me be the first to tell you, you will only experience personal growth if you are confident in taking chances. I took the opportunity and risked my comfort zone as a second-grade teacher because someone saw my leadership potential. At the time, I didn't see it in myself. That same year, my principal decided to make me chairperson of the school's Student Council body, which consists of grades 3, 4, & 5. Because I was willing to move up and teach another grade level, other opportunities started to present their way to me. Don't be afraid to take that chance when new opportunities are presented.

Since I was now departmentalized, I had a partner teacher who taught other subjects like Language Arts and Social Studies. After working alone, without a partner teacher for the beginning of my career, having a partner was a challenge; I was used to having one hundred percent control over my student's learning patterns. I have learned that any relationship or involvement in working with another person will test your patience to see how well you work with others. Because I will share my students with another teacher, we had to agree and have the same mental approach: putting our students' needs first. Throughout my teaching career, I have been truly fortunate to work alongside four talented teaching partners, all of whom have brought different skill sets that complement each other—special shout out to them all: Mrs. Wilkendorf, Mr. Barzar, Ms. Dixon, and Ms. McDaniel.

Being on the third-grade team, I have also worked with fantastic teachers with different personalities and wit. We've planned lessons together, orchestrated field trips and extracurricular programs, and participated in multiple fundraising

THE FOURTH FRUIT

activities for our students. We were a united team. A team that was always unified for the betterment of our grade level and students. But when the pressure of state testing rolled around the corner, then things quickly shifted. It's funny how everyone can work together well: bounce ideas, share strategies, and co-teach a lesson without complaining. But as soon as the state results are in, everyone is comparing scores, seeing how students did on the test, talking about other teachers in their performance...the list goes on and on. Does this sound like anyone in your circle? Our union quickly became a unit of one once the scores were in. In all honesty, going through those ups and downs of working with a partner and with a group of teachers helped me understand the importance and value of teamwork. When a team comes together for the greater good, their support can boost morale on a job site. Even though we worked collaboratively on achieving the same goal, we were still individual teachers (people) with self-motivating goals that only one could accomplish. The weight of others' influential thoughts and actions substantially impacted my first year as a third-grade state testing teacher.

In third grade, students are required to take a state test focusing on math and reading skills. This is the first year they are introduced to a state exam on this magnitude level. The pressure and standards are high for everyone: students, parents, teachers, and administrative staff. Because of the high expectations, the optimism of succeeding in those expectations can be fearsome for anyone affected.

At the beginning of each school year, each teacher sits with the principal or their appraiser leader (most of the time, it's your principal) to set goals for the upcoming school year. In the appraisal meeting, the expectation is to discuss the teacher's plan of action for the learning success of their students. Each teacher is entitled to determine how well their students will perform on the End of the Year (EOY) assessments. Whether the assessment is state or district level, everyone must be accountable. Since it was my first year in a testing grade, I decided to get input from my team members on my percentage rate. The percentage rate is based on the predicted number of students passing the state test, given a specific passing grade score. Because we live in a realistic world and tend to go off facts and not solely off theory. I wanted my predicted rate to be as close to factual as possible. I also wanted to be reasonable. Therefore, I took the advice of my team members, which informed me that not every student would pass the state test, and that's just the reality. They advised me not to put extra pressure on myself with a ridiculous passing percentage number. My coworkers stated that 60% is ideal and 70% means you were pushing it. I was appalled to think that's kind of low. Still, maybe they're right because I never taught a testing grade and based on the Academic Excellence Indicator System (AEIS) report, no one at that campus made 100% before, not even at the district level. Considering those numbers, I decided to set my goal at 80%. I went into the appraisal meeting with the goal in mind. Of course, some of my colleagues laughed at my high number, but I wanted to be optimistic and hope for the best.

I didn't want to be a cruel teacher (person) and set my standards of my student's performance level too low, not showing affection for how well they would do. I wanted to put my number at 100%, but I didn't want to come off as arrogant. If you believe in your work, why should you set low expectations based on another's opinion?

The day of receiving the scores had finally arrived. Everyone rushed into the principal chamber to see how well they did. I was a little late getting in there due to after-school duty, but when

PATIENCE

I did arrive, my Assistant Principal was all smiles and congratulated me on my student's results. He said that 78% of my students passed the test. I was delighted to hear the great news, but in my mind, I was like, darn, I missed my goal by 2 pts. The Assistant Principal then said I had one of the highest scores in my grade level. I was shocked and puzzled! The new teacher in this testing world just received the highest score amongst her team. I later discovered I was top five in my district for third-grade math scores. I didn't know whether to be excited or concerned; after all, it wasn't 100%. I knew 78% was not a high score, and to be top five with that score was a little disappointing.

The level of expectation from the state requirements can be challenging for most nine-year-old, especially those with little English literacy living in states closer to the border.

To give you a little insight on what a 3rd grade math state testing day looks like, back when I was teaching: The test is roughly four hours long with approximately a hundred math word problem questions. Imagine yourself solving and showing your work on all one hundred-word problems. The thought alone is daunting. You are in a silent room for four hours without disruption, interference, or guidance to help you complete the exam. You must rely on the best knowledge of what you learned throughout the year. You are not allowed to use any notes or books to help assist if you get stuck or confused. You can only rely on the strategies you've learned through memory. You can only raise your hand if you need another pencil, tissue paper, or a restroom break. If you get done early or before the exam window time is up, you can put your head down, nap, or read a pre-selected book that's not correlated to the exam. By painting this picture in your mind, I hope to give you a little insight into what testing days look like for a nine-year-old student. This type of preparation for an exam can be very intense for students, parents, teachers, and administrators.

I am not trying to justify the validity of the outcome test scores, but the reality is this is what the education system looks like today. It's disheartening to know that percentile rankings of a systematic state exam measure our student's achievement success. However, this systematic data did help dissect the information needed to get to the root cause, identifying the learning gaps.

I needed to understand how to use the data to effectively plan relevant lessons for my students and my grade level. Those planned lessons, now applicable to students' learning, led me to join the district math curriculum team. As I mentioned in chapter 1, there weren't any teacher notes or scripts for new teachers. The only thing that was provided, at the time, was the state's essentials and knowledge standards performance requirements. But as things were shifting due to data and performance levels, the district wanted more input from highly qualified teachers who successfully made incremental progress with their student's learning. When asked to be part of this initiative, the math curriculum team developed the *Curriculum Writing Cadre*. I was honored for the opportunity to help new teachers grow and expand in their delivery of how they instruct their lessons. As highly qualified teachers, we were now establishing teacher note scripts based on our own experience and the success we were having in the classrooms for those new teachers who were starting to onboard in education.

A quote states, "When you are not sharing your brilliant ideas, you are doing a disservice to others"[9].

---

[9] Inspirational Quote by Angela Maiers

THE FOURTH FRUIT

The same year, I was nominated with the title "Houston Area Alliance of Black School Educators," known as HAABSE, Teacher of the Year. It was an honor to be recognized not just at my campus and school district but also in my community and city. In my same modest mindset of receiving the Rookie Teacher of the Year, again, I didn't expect it, and I'm sure others deserved the title. This award from HAABSE, a great organization to be a part of, meant significant gratitude for serving my community. Its mission is to enhance the education of all students and to exercise leadership in providing valuable professional services and strategies to institutions, agencies, and communities engaged in creating an environment where students, particularly black students, can achieve academic excellence. Receiving this award was one of the most rewarding recognitions I could ever imagine. Once I was honored with this award, my principal encouraged me to continue my education by working on my master's degree, which I eventually did.

It was now year three for me in education, and I was starting to feel pretty good and pumped about my decision to become a teacher. As an educator, I was walking in my purpose and calling in life. Knowing I was making a difference outside my household and that my voice was being heard felt good. Because of my innovative and creative skills, I was asked to create a school brochure along with inputs for revising the campus mission statement since the school was approaching its 30th anniversary. At this time in my career, I received a few more recognitions and awards for my performance and leadership skills. I was now indulging in the highlights of my career, and it felt amazing.

Those recognitions and awards were a part of the harvest I had reaped. I planted the seeds way before taking those first steps into my classroom. It felt wonderful to be recognized for the work I was doing. But it was not the "end" all result of the work I still needed to accomplish. If someone has never told you before, let me be the first to say having some sort of recognition and receiving different types of awards are all wonderful when you reap the benefits of sowing seeds into the life of others. But you must be careful not to stay up too high in all the edification and pride of what you have accomplished. God humorously shows you that even the highest can be knocked down off their chariot.

THE FOURTH FRUIT

Nevertheless, God does want you to enjoy all your successes, recognitions, awards, promotions, etc. If you earned or worked for it, then be blissful in it. You were awarded a deserved accomplishment, and it's okay to celebrate. But remain humble, and don't forget where you came from. Don't allow those thoughts to convince you that you are now better than others around you because you were recognized with a special award.

Keep in mind that rewards will come and go, but relationships that were built will last forever.

I was now entering my fourth year as a teacher, my second year teaching a state testing grade. The state testing window was fast approaching the corner, but I wasn't too nervous this time since I had accomplished it the first time. I had rehearsed the same speech that I would give my appraiser, with a goal of 80% to pass the test. As the testing window was closing, I was now sitting on numerous committees as a member or chairperson. My head was swell (pumped with high amounts of arrogance), and my coworkers could see how my demeanor was changing rapidly. I tried to act humble but was a bit snobbish at times. I started to notice some of my team members not coming to me for advice and not sharing their strategies or ideas, but in those moments, I didn't care because I knew I was good at what I did, and that's all that mattered.

I was now put in a position where my status was placed on a pedestal, and I felt untouchable. I had let those awards and recognition be superior to my true purpose for becoming a teacher. I had to stop and pause to think about where I was and why I was doing the things I was doing. Sometimes in life, you must go back to remind yourself of how you got to where you are. Somewhere in between receiving those acknowledgments, I lost my purpose. My head was so high in the clouds that I couldn't see there was a storm coming. That storm resulted in receiving my second round of test scores.

Now that we had made it around to testing, it was time again when the test scores were in. The moment of truth when teachers would hold their breath to find out how well the students did. It was the same procedure; everyone went into the principal office to see how they did. Again, test scores are in; this time, I had the lowest performing numbers ...63% passed. Oh Lord, what had happened? I was in disbelief! I just knew it was a mix-up, and my scores were skewed or tampered with. I knew this couldn't be right. I was unwilling to accept those scores and started playing the blame game and not owning up to my actions and faults. I blamed it on doing too many extracurricular activities, working on my master's degree, and writing math lessons for the district; I even put some of the blame on my husband and kids (they didn't have anything to do with my students' learning abilities). I was embarrassed by the percentage and humiliated by my title as a "Highly Qualified" teacher.

At that moment, the success of getting those awards felt like a massive disappointment because I wasn't living up to the titles I once received.

There will be moments when things are going so well that you will allow the celebratory moments to oversee the real reason you were celebrating. Don't lose focus (your purpose) and forget the plan (your calling). Don't let yourself get distracted with multiple tasks, titles, and side jobs that will make you lose focus on the main objective.

Scientists say, "light travels in a straight line." If your goal is to be a light with hope, then don't stray away. My intention wasn't to wander. I just let other things cloud my vision. I could no longer see the straight line in the clouds of self-glorification I allowed myself to remain in. I shifted my focus off my purpose to try to figure out why other people weren't achieving success in their classrooms. I figured if I could do it, they should be able to succeed at a reasonable rate with attainable goals. Sometimes we get too focused on other people's business or try to get into other people's lane while getting off track with our own doings. I had let my focus shift from student to self and (others).

I was living in the ego of self-satisfaction with what I had done versus what I still needed to do. Not only did I let myself down, but I also let those who believed in me, especially my students. This was a BIG wake-up call for self-reflection!

Note to Self-Reflect:

This chapter heavily talked about reaping the benefits of one's harvest. It was important for me to share the insights of this particular time frame as a teacher. I wanted the reader to know how crucial it is to remain humble once you have been rewarded with certain acknowledgments in life. When you find your purpose, focus on why it became your purpose, to begin with. Don't get sidetracked by things that will make you lose your focus. For example, If your calling is to teach in an education system, don't be one of those teachers who only enjoy the benefits of working only nine months out of the year while having a summer break and every holiday off. Those are good benefits of being a teacher, but they shouldn't be a selling point of why you want to be a teacher. Your true purpose in life will not be limited to an "on" and "off" season. Instead, it will be a daily habit of wanting to do greatness in the lives of others.

Reaping your harvest from time to time can be enjoyable, especially if you laid out the seeds from the beginning. But try not to stay too long in that season of reaping your own harvest. It might be enjoyable for you, but what about those around you? Be careful who you are willing to share and celebrate your success with. Not everyone around you might not be in a celebratory mood, especially if they are not succeeding. Once your seed has been achieved, then keep planting new seeds. While planting those new seeds, remember not to shout to the world about your doings. Sometimes the biggest harvests are the ones whose work has been done in silence.

Over your lifespan, career or personal, think of a time when you were most proud of an accomplishment you achieved. How did it make you feel not knowing you would receive it? Did you celebrate and then move on, or did you bash in your glory of success and forget you still had work to do? Write down the big highlights of your life that made you want to continue to learn and grow. If those highlighted moments were little incremental progress, write it down as a self-congratulatory moment.

As stated before, having an incremental appreciation of progress is good, and it should be worth a pause of celebration. Celebrate yourself if no one is willing to stop and acknowledge what you are doing. It's okay to pat yourself on the back from time to time. Every human being wants to feel accepted and loved at some point in their life. But once you get that acceptance, award, or recognition for whatever it is you seek, don't let it be your stopping point. Even when you have reached everything you wanted to accomplish, you still must maintain a sense of humility and a sense of modesty to keep learning and growing. The longer you live, the more it's crucial to stay assertive in the current changes in your life. Instead, look at it as a pivot point in your life, a place of reflection and an opportunity to build upon.

My husband and I constantly seek the latest inventions to stay abreast of the trends. We do it not necessarily to be a part of the worldly doings, but instead, we want to remain relevant in today's society.

To keep your harvest going, you must know what new seeds are out there to be planted. You should always put yourself in a position that will allow you to grow and make a difference in the world.

Let's take a moment to assess what harvest you are currently reaping. First, have you thought about the harvest you are presently in? Are you now in a position allowing you to continue learning, growing, and planting new seeds? If so, then do you like what you have harvested? If you do not like the harvest you are reaping, it may be time to check the seed you are sowing.

Don't let your last award stop you from learning and growing. As long as you breathe, you can still define or redefine your purpose in life. **When you vow to live in your purpose, you are planting seeds into the lives of others, not just your own.** The harvest is for others to benefit from and for you to sow. People who do their job get a paycheck, but advocates who fight for what's right receive accolades; their names will always be remembered because of the humbleness and gratitude they gave.

Regardless of what field or career you may be in now or about to enter, keep in mind there will always be room for growth and improvement. As a person living in their purpose, you should always reflect on what worked well to produce good results. As time progresses and the world changes with new innovations and a new generation to lead, so will your heart and mind. Your willingness to have an open mindset and to see others' viewpoints will be one step towards reaching and impacting another's life.

During 2020, everyone had a moment to think and reflect on life, family, friends, and loved ones. That was a monumental time frame with many people thinking about their future and lives. Many people were questioning their life purpose and even second-guessing their chosen careers. Many people were forced to bear the fruit of patience with unforeseen layoffs, furloughs, and unemployment. It was a year when we ALL had to demonstrate patience. Because there was nothing anyone could do to make this virus disappear, everyone had to endure the moment. Even if you were not a person with patience, you

THE FOURTH FRUIT

still had to be capable of accepting or tolerating delay, trouble, or suffering without getting angry or upset. It was a markable time that many will not forget. My condolences are to those who have lost everything that year. And I am here to tell you, with a bit of hope and faith, you can believe that God still has a purpose for your life. You can keep planting seeds even when faced with uncertainties and doubts. Just continue to be patient, wait, and watch the fruits of your labor begin to prosper.

While you are in the waiting and watching period of your life, remember that time is a process you will go through. Your life is not meant to be stuck in the waiting storm; eventually, you will come out from that waiting time into a season of greatness. Use that time to sow seeds into the lives of others and then watch your harvest grow into a field of abundant fruits. Your rewards will reflect how kind-hearted you are to others. Now that you have learned how to embrace the wait time of patience and see your harvest reaping with good benefits, let's continue empowering others by lifting them with kindness.

Kindness

The Fifth Fruit

Chapter 5:

Dress for Success.
Clothe yourself with *KINDNESS*.

"She is clothed in strength and dignity"
—Proverbs 31:25-26

As a little girl, Sunday was my favorite day of the week. It was the day we went to church and returned to a Sunday soul food dinner waiting at the house. It was also a day when all the family (aunts, uncles, and cousins) would come together to meet and fellowship, almost like a mini-family reunion. Sunday was when my mom dressed my sisters and I in cute little tutu dresses and big ribbon bows to match. Sunday was fashion day because it was church day, and everyone wore their best Sunday outfits. Husbands and wives coordinated their outfits; the elderly gentlemen wore the brightest three-piece suits (and matching shoes), the older ladies wore big hats which

KINDNESS

blocked everyone's view, and the little children all wore their best outfits. In my culture, wearing your best to attend church signifies respect for God's house. That meant you took the church and the message very seriously. Everyone respected one another and greeted each other with love and affirmation. Wearing tacky clothes or everyday casual wear wasn't quite fitting for the house of God as I knew it. I know the Bible verse that says," ...come as you are", but that verse was about spiritual issues, not your wardrobe. When Sunday morning came around to go to church, my family and I were ready to put on our best garments for the house of God.

As I mentioned in the previous chapter, when you put on your best, you put on a sense of empowerment that no one can take away from you. Your best may come in the form of a smile, attitude, cologne, body spray, clothes, shoes & jewelry. People respect you more when you look presentable because it shows you care enough about yourself to take the time to dress the part, whatever that part may be at that moment. Dressing the part gives you not only a sense of empowerment but also a sense of pride, knowing you are putting your best foot forward to gain the awareness you are seeking.

In childhood, most people would play dress-up to mimic someone or something they wanted to be or accomplish. Playing dress-up may have given them the confidence they needed to imagine themself as that person. I, too, had those childlike moments of pretending to be certain people when I grew up. I wanted to be a doctor, an entrepreneur, and a teacher. I had always admired the work ethic each of these careers had to offer. And as I grew in age, I was fortunate enough to be a part of all three entities.

My first college degree was an Associate Degree in medical science. I obtained this degree before I became a housewife. I wanted to practice medicine on a nurse practitioner level at the time. I was always fascinated with the anatomy of the human body and all the different types of herbal medicine that helps to heal the body. However, once I received my degree, I wasn't sure if that was what I wanted to do. As I was getting a feel for the field before pursuing a B.A. in nursing, I applied to work at a medical clinic in a small town in Louisiana. I loved my job. I loved everything about it, including the staff, the patients, and the pharmaceutical sales representative (who always gave us freebies). The pharmaceutical sales rep were the people who educated you on the new types of pills and other medicines that were up and coming.

Working in the medical field, dressing a certain way was imperative to the job duty. As a medical assistant working alongside doctors and nurse practitioners, I had to dress suitably for the tasks given to me. In that was dressing in scrubs. I had to wear scrubs daily with no other options. In this work environment, wearing scrubs was one of the most comfortable pieces of garment anyone would want to wear. It consists of a linen top and drawstring linen bottoms. And the good part is you don't have to iron it. Besides wearing scrubs, other restrictions were a part of the dress code, like no open-toe shoes, sandals, or dressy shoes. Tennis shoes were the only shoes you could wear for safety reasons. Wearing scrubs and tennis shoes sounds like the perfect outfit to wear daily in this type of high-function work environment. But other items were restricted, such as perfume, artificial nails or nail polish, excessive hairstyles, and no jewelry was allowed. Being the girly girl I am, not being able to wear these things was a little disappointing. But if I wanted to be a part of this work environment, giving up these dispensable items was mandatory. Dressing the role of a medical assistant allowed me to be swift with corresponding to the urgency of the patient's needs. It was the dress code for medical work, and there was no way of getting around it. Wearing this type of garment with these types of restrictions made me, and those working in the field, look professional for this line of work. As medical professionals, it is pivotal to dress the required part.

In most professions, if not all, a dress code is required to fit a job description. The reason for a specific dress code is to portray an ethical standard that a person holds. In addition, doing so shows the knowledge and skills that one has learned through education and training at a high level and who is prepared to apply this knowledge and exercise these skills in the interest of others. That said, it is important to "dress the part" in the line of work you are conducting. In my years of education, I have seen many teachers who show up to work lacking self-confidence and work attire awareness. As an educator, dressing for success in any grade level means conducting oneself responsibly, with integrity, accountability, and excellence. It's the type of professional attire that all should expect.

When I started seeking a teaching position in the public school district, I had my first interview

KINDNESS

with a lady named Helen Livers. Helen was more than a phenomenal leader who served in her community for over three decades. But she was a benevolent advocate for public education. She has extraordinary poise when she walks into a room, owning everyone's presence. She is one lady who always and still today dresses the part of a leader and former principal. Her style was never flashy but instead very classy and sophisticated. She always wore her Sunday best every day as a principal, with the hairdo and polished nails. I never once saw her with flat shoes, nevertheless tennis shoes. As the younger generation would say, she was on point every 365 days of the year, dressing the part of a school leader. And I'm forever grateful to have had the opportunity to work under her leadership for four straight years leading up to her retirement. Even though she did not have all the answers when leading our school campus and culture, her presence and demeanor made it seem like she did. She was highly respected by those she directly influenced and those who didn't have a personal relationship with her. They respected her because of her charisma and ability to make others feel valued.

It was important for me to highlight Helen's attributes, just like the woman in Proverbs 31, because she is a woman of today's society who is clothed with kindness. She is leading a legacy of honor that proves other women can lead, not just a school community but any leadership position, with confidence knowing others will respect their work. In any profession, one would want their colleagues, peers, and students to give them the level of respect that is quite deserving. Mostly every human wants to be honored with care and the warm love of approval. Showing a sign of gratitude, politeness, empathy for differences, active listening, serving others, or apologizing when wrong are all ways one can demonstrate when displaying respect.

As parents, we teach our children to respect their elders. Similarly, we show them how to care and be kind to others. This level of respect is universal and applies to the teacher-student relationship. There is a certain respect level a child should have for an adult. However, some adults expect respect from others while at the same time not providing the necessary tools needed for others to succeed in life. For example, educators should meet students on a level where they can relate to their students and understand their academic needs. By doing so, the student will want to rise to their teacher's expectations;

by showing respect to them. As an educator, I believe in having fun with my students, having little conversations with them, playing ball, or even attending one of their games or concerts. Students will feel appreciated knowing their teacher cares enough to do the small things in life that can make the most significant impact later. While it is essential for teachers to meet students on their academic level, it is equally important to have boundaries when building this teacher-student relationship.

My values as a teacher are to be kind and friendly to all those, including those students who may not be under your leadership. Being kind and friendly shows a level of mutual respect. A type of respect that can't be displayed in your physical appearance but inwardly, within your spiritual being. Your spiritual well-being relates to your sense of life's meaning and your purpose. It is the inner attire in you that shows your confidence, positivity, humbleness, gratitude, warmth, compassion, and excitement to see others prosper in their success. These are the best pieces of garments anyone should want to wear, especially if you are seeking a level of respect. Whatever your title in life, wearing your daily spiritual attire will lead you to a life filled with gratitude.

THE FIFTH FRUIT

The best type of clothes to put on include but is not limited to *love, joy, peace, patience, kindness, goodness, faithfulness, gentleness, and self-control* [10]. These types of clothes are free at no cost and with no taxes added to them. You don't have to pay for delivery or wait for it to be in stock. You just have to be willing to open your heart and mind. Be open to sharing, sending, and receiving the fruits that make life enjoyable. Sometimes you don't have to search for your purpose in life because it is a part of you. You just have to wear that spiritual attire fitting for your well-being, and then the rest is history. When you get dressed to walk into your purpose, other people's perceptions of you will not matter. You will have the necessary garments to overcome self-doubt, and your dreams of possibilities will turn into realities.

While envisioning the woman I wanted to be, I also had to imagine dressing like her. I knew I had to dress the part before getting the part. Therefore, I created an image in my mind and the different characteristics I would have to embody if I wanted to become that person. Only I had the power to bring that person alive. While believing in myself and staying motivated to achieve

---
[10] Fruits of the Spirit, Galatians 5:22

greatness, I had not to let self-doubt take over who I wanted to be. Self-doubt is characterized by uncertainty regarding one or more aspects of the self. It is something that everyone may experience at certain times in their lives. However, you may need more tools to overcome when self-doubt becomes debilitating.

I often felt unmotivated and drained, not wanting to do anything or be optimistic. Those days when I was unsure of my being, and my purpose in life, I had to remind myself of the love God had given me. HIS love was the tool I needed to justify my life, filling me with hope for the future. This type of love pushes through low self-esteem and self-doubt of thinking I was not worthy of being someone. Once I reassured myself that I was worthy, more positive thoughts started to generate. And the more willpower I had to be motivated and activated. I had to put on the characteristics of what God had equipped me to be; the person I was called to be.

The book of Ephesians, chapter 6, verse 11, references putting on the "Armor of God." It states, "To put the whole armor of God, so you may be able to stand firm against the tactics of the devil" [11]. As a biblical reference, this metaphor

---

[11] Armor of God, Ephesians 6:11

THE FIFTH FRUIT

may refer to physical armor worn by God in metaphorical battles or too vigilant righteousness in general as bestowed by the grace of God. It was meant for the knights to be equipped with protection against their enemies. Paul references it as a spiritual warfare, stating that we should clothe ourselves with the: belt of truth, the breastplate of righteousness, feet fitted with the gospel of peace, shield ourselves with faith, the helmet of salvation, and the sword of the spirit.

When the enemy tries to make you think you are not worthy and your life has no purpose, then this is the moment to seek God for strength, courage, and boldness so you can walk in power knowing your purpose is full of worth in your life and the lives of others.

Whether it's your Sunday's best or just another workday in your professional field, it is time to wear your best inward garments to show who you are. Yes, it is important to "dress the part" of whatever your title may hold. But it is paramount that your spiritual attire will always outshine your physical garments. Be conscious of what garments you are wearing while activating your purpose. You want to make sure your wardrobe is always in sync.

Note to Self-Reflect:

This chapter discusses dressing for success while clothing yourself in kindness. Even though we know kindness is not a physical garment, it's a behavior, a quality of being. It is important to always display it. You can dress in the most luxurious clothes or the most fabulous latest fashion, but those garments will not get you the peace or happiness you desire. You only get that enjoyment when you mentally allow yourself to be free of the label others have bestowed on you. You are the only person who can label yourself based on your attitude and how you feel about life.

Living a life full of kindful thoughts will have you looking and feeling your best. Your outer garments will not matter as much as what people will see, which will be a kind-hearted spirit.

Spiritually thinking, not physical appearance, what type of clothes do you have in your armoire, your closet? Is your closet full of doubt, worrying, complaining, or mean- spirit? Be true to yourself when reflecting on these questions. You may see yourself as one way, but how do you treat others around you? Take a moment to self-reflect on what you are wearing and how you are portraying yourself in public when everyone is watching and in private (when it's just you and the mirror). You just might surprise yourself with who you really are.

When you think about your purpose and calling, write down how you will dress for your success. Are you going to choose the uplifting garments or the garments that will tear down a life? Spiritually speaking, will your garments have stains, holes, tears, bleach, or any unpleasant distress? These are all questions to self-reflect on what you have been putting on daily. Remember, you can encourage and motivate others, not just through what you say but by how you live your life. True character is who you are when no one is around. It's your daily habits, your beliefs, your ethics, and your morals that come deeply within yourself. People will look up to you as a role model when you are true to yourself. They will want to mimic your style and have the same, if not similar, charisma you put out, which is good. Your goal will be for others to spread the same kindness and generosity you are planting.

You will become a walking billboard with an inspiring and motivating message. People will see you in a different light, and goodness and mercy will follow you.

Goodness

The Sixth Fruit

Chapter 6:

Moving On. *GOODNESS* and Mercy will follow you.

As the years went by and my students were growing up as young adolescents moving from primary to intermediate to middle school age, so was my plan as an educator. At this time, I had finished my master's degree in educational leadership and was ready to take my career to the next level. The principal, at the time, had always seen value in her staff and wanted the best for all of us. She was willing to invest in whatever was necessary to see her staff grow as educators. She always had a heart of compassion to see others succeed in their journey. She would push me into leadership roles each year, assigning me as head chair of extracurricular activities. She would inform me of the different cohort leadership programs that were taking place in the district so I could take part in them. She uplifted and inspired me to work on a master's degree in education, motivating me to teach at a testing grade level and even taking me under her wing as a principalship intern. Her motto was for me to think outside the box, making the impossible possible. She wanted me to think "what if" and not "if I only can" thoughts. She had high hopes and expectations of me as a teacher and leader. And I was determined not to let her down.

In 2014, when she announced her retirement, I was sad to see her go but also happy for her. I was her protégé, a person who is guided and supported by an older, more experienced, influential person. I had looked up to her as a role model for the past four years, and now it was time for her to move on. Many teachers talked about moving to another school or district or shifting careers that year. The retention rate dropped the following year significantly as the new principal came on. Her retirement made me realize the substantial mark great leaders can leave on a place when they have put in good work. If you are in a stage where you feel you are being called to another place or to spread your service elsewhere, make sure to leave with grace, knowing the work

THE SIXTH FRUIT

you have put in will not go unnoticed. The best time to soar to the next big thing is when you have excelled in your current position. Just because you've been to a job site for a while doesn't mean you were meant for leadership at that place. Some places are just temporary positions for growth and learning, nothing more. You must know when it's your time to go.

Many people get confused or upset when a person in good leadership leaves. Some people are so complacent with their current administration that they are unwilling to accept new leadership. True leaders don't quit or leave because they feel like it. They leave because their purpose is sometimes bigger than self. Once you have outgrown a position, whether winning or losing, you must progress to the next chapter of your life. Not everyone will understand your decision at first, but you can rest in knowing you did what was meant during the time and with the responsibility given to you. While some people are there to pave the way for others, it doesn't mean they are there to stay forever.

I have seen new teachers who strived to be just like seasoned teachers throughout my career.

People who are seasoned in their careers have been doing that line of work for a long time. They have laid the foundation of learning, growing, and achieving the goals they had set out since day one. In other words, they planted their seeds at the beginning of their career, and now they are reaping the harvest, while some people who are starting their career desire immediate success. Nothing is wrong with visualizing your success based on another person's success. The only issue is not knowing what a person has sacrificed or endured to get to that fruitful life you are now seeing. The harvest you will reap will depend on the seeds you will plant.

When starting a new role or having new leadership to guide you, be mindful of the pros and cons of the new territory.

An advantage for some people might be the fresh start they were looking for with new leadership. While a disadvantage for another person might be a restarting point to reprove the success they once have mastered to the previous leader. Sometimes in life, your resume can be great to show all the things you have accomplished. But having a resume alone will sometimes not be enough.

I recently attended a women's conference at my church where we had a guest speaker, Michelle Thorton, Black Entertainment Television (BET) network vice president. She made a great point when she said, "If you had to send God your resume would He give you the job?". She had me thinking about my personal life, not just my professional life. I asked myself, would God hire me based on my many deeds? I had to look closely at what I had on my resume that made me a qualified person of interest. I had to self-reflect to see if my work was enough to get me to the next level in life.

For me having a new principal meant shifting my mindset. All I had accomplished during the first four years as an educator didn't mean anything to her because she wasn't a part of my story at the time. Up to that point, the work I had achieved had felt wasted. In my mind, I believed she would have no interest in what I had done. Therefore, as a teacher with four years of experience, I felt like I was back to square one, trying to prove to my new principal that I would go the extra mile for my students' academic learning.

When you have planted good seeds and given them all the essentials for them to grow, you will not need approval or affirmation from others. I had let deceptive thoughts overshadow the work that I had already done. I had to reassure myself that my work was not for others' liking but to glorify what God had called me to do.

Throughout my first year of working under this new leadership, my new principal saw the excellent work that I was doing. This dedication led me to be named HAABSE teacher of the year for the second time, but this time under new leadership. She saw the greatness in me and my work, but my resume still couldn't help me get to the next level of where I wanted to be on campus. That year was my last year servicing at the school/district. It was my home for five years, the making and beginning of my career as an educator. My time there had come to an end. And it was now time for me to move on.

There will be moments when you will find yourself in a rut. A place where you can't grow, not because you are not getting the resources or nutrition you need, but because the pot you sit in is now too small. When my husband and I bought our first home, it was perfect. It was just the amount of space we needed for our growing family. But then the years passed, and our kids grew up from babies to children and now teenagers. As much as our house was the perfect home, it was getting too small for our family's needs. In all cases, just like my perfect house, your current pot will not change; it's just a shell. But as you become wiser and more knowledgeable about understanding your calling, you will eventually grow to a point where you can't fit in the pot anymore.

Sometimes God will put you in place for a reason or a season, even if it looks like hell. You may not understand at the very moment why you have been placed in a particular location, but as you continue to learn and grow, you will realize your purpose and place. Moving on for some people might be the best thing to happen to them. Moving on can bring pain, trouble, turmoil, or even disappointment to others. My mom would say that if you are not coming out of a storm, you are going into one. Life is beautiful, but that doesn't mean it will always bring beauty. You will face hardship from time to time. You will have the power to determine how you will respond or react to those difficult moments when they do come.

In November 2000, I lost my sister LaTyra to a horrific car accident. She would have been 23 years old the following month. It was a sudden, unexpected death. What made it much worse for our family was that my dad witnessed the whole thing at first sight. He tried to pull her out of the car, but she was jammed there. Her head was under the steering wheel (attached) but broken. Seeing her lifeless body was unbearable. It was a day that would never be forgotten. It took the coroner a while to get to the scene and pronounce her dead. The whole town was out watching the scene as we tried to save her, but there was nothing we could've done. It was too late. This experience was the worst my family and I had ever gone through. It was heartbreaking to watch my sister taken that quickly and that young. She had a one-year-old daughter at the time. It took months of counseling and healing to get past that moment. But during it all, we knew we had to move on. Moving on didn't mean we forgot her or stopped thinking about all the good memories we shared. Moving on meant we had to keep living to tell her story, her story as a mother, daughter, and friend. We had to keep her memories alive.

Moving on can be challenging, but at the same time, it can be an outlet to keep growing and pushing yourself to be an asset to others.

You will never know when you will find that breakthrough in life if you don't keep trying or moving toward growth. For some people, staying in one place might be ideal or their final place until retirement. If you choose to stay, then it's okay. But what is not okay is staying at a place or location and not growing and learning. You can only reap the benefits of your harvest by constantly applying yourself to new things. In most situations, you are not living purposefully when you are not growing or trying new things. To deactivate your purpose is to be ineffective in your calling in life. Never let your circumstance, whether your age, gender, culture, or economic status, stop you from learning, growing, and reaping the good you have acquired. Daily learning will expand your mind and open your heart for more love to pour in and out. Your goal will always be wanting to gain more, so you can give more.

Note to Self-Reflect:

If you see yourself as a leader in your future, whether in your career or personal life, make sure you bring on skill sets and good qualities that can be added to what's already in place. No need to

GOODNESS

reinvent the wheels or start from scratch when progress is already in place. Great leaders before your time have sacrificed and laid the foundation for future leaders like yourself to continue to pave the way. Just as your mom, grandmother, and other ancestors had laid a foundation for your family, so will you when it comes to you leading others.

Shifting your mind for a moment, I want you to think of a recipe your grandma, mom, or auntie created that was known as the family's favorite dish recipe. I'm sure you can think of some memorable dish you long to fix for yourself or your family. As the recipe is handed or passed down, you may add a little salt, throw in a bay leaf for decoration, or even use a different brand of milk. Adding those few ingredients didn't change the whole dish; you just modified the taste slightly. The point is the recipe still holds the main ingredients, but with little accommodations or modifications you add, it now makes you a part of the recipe. Remaining humble and appreciative of the foundation set in place will lead you to a more excellent cornerstone for the next generation.

Remember that you are also planting new seeds when starting a new chapter in your life.

Starting anything new will be challenging until you get the hang of things. Just as flowers don't grow overnight, so won't the seeds you will plant at the beginning. Albert Einstein said: "A person who never made a mistake never tried anything new." Think about that quote for a moment. Have you made any mistakes or made any wrong moves in your life? Or better yet, when did you last take the courage to start something new and exciting?

When I moved on, I didn't know what my future would look like or entail. I wasn't sure if the grass would be greener on the other side of the field. I just wanted to keep growing, living, and planting seeds.

If you have done all you could and still see no growth in your life or career, you will know it is time to make a big move. You must take the initial step and put your foot forward to unroot yourself from your position. Just as a tree can be uprooted and replanted in another location, so can you. You must believe that there is a bigger plan for your calling in life. **Once you start to see the cracks of your pot breaking, it is time for you to be replanted in a bigger pot.**

GOODNESS

There will be moments when you will have to justify to others that you are the right person for the job or that career you seek. When doing so, you must stand your ground to show this is where you should be. Your resume may not get you to the next level. You will have to sacrifice your time, energy, and resources if you want to excel. You must be open-minded when changes affect the soil you are sowing your seeds.

Unexpected changes can sometimes derail you from where you want to be. Those changes might come in the form of new people in your life or new procedures or protocols you have to adhere to. It may even come in the form of a tragic loss. Whatever the changes, don't let those circumstances doubt your capabilities of what you can achieve. Your work and great deeds will show for themselves. People will notice your effort, and your success will speak volumes. Don't let your accomplishments be the final print on your resume. Continue to seek all opportunities, even when it seems to be a mistake.

Goodness and Mercy will follow you wherever you may go. You will continue to plant many seeds in different locations. Don't be tricked into staying in a position or place where you have

THE SIXTH FRUIT

outgrown your harvest. There will be many other opportunities to inspire others. You must have faith knowing your journey has not ended. And it's just the beginning of seeing the fruits of your labor.

Once your fruits have fully outgrown from one harvest to the next, other people will want to seek your advice because of your obedience and faithfulness to stand firm in your purpose. Your courageous move toward your goal will empower others to do the same.

Faithfulness

The Seventh Fruit

Chapter 7:

Sister Talk. FAITHFULNESS to empower others.

"Sisters are different flowers from the same garden."
—*Unknown*

Back in my childhood days, I had a group of neighborhood friends who would get together just about every day after school. We would ride our bikes together or sit on the train tracks and talk about life all day, especially in the summertime. Since our parents had all worked at the same place of employment, our schedule to hang out together was always synchronized. Looking back, I appreciate those moments as a child. Those were the good old days when everyone would freely express their opinions, and no one would get upset if they didn't agree with one another.

Nowadays, people can't have opinions without the other person being offended. Back then, having an opinion was a hidden way of telling the other person the truth about themself but in a non-judgmental way. The stories we shared as friends were incredible and, at the same time, enjoyable. It was a great feeling to know you were being heard, even if the message you were trying to convey didn't make any sense. In those moments, no one cared about the made-up tales or the boisterous drama that was told because we all knew they were telling a fib. But we laughed and enjoyed the stories anyway. It felt good to be in the presence of others with the same interest or at least the same level of compassion to care about your interest. It made me feel important and visible, but for the most part, it made me feel like I was not alone.

We live in a BIG world where many people now share the same interests as others. Nowadays, it's normal to run into someone with the same calling and desires you may have. Sharing similar traits of another person's purpose can bring about a more significant cause. However, it can be challenging to connect with that person when they don't live nearby. But today, social media makes it a little easier to communicate with other people who may live far away. Because people are now vulnerable to sharing their stories online, those reading them tend to feel a part of it. Especially if the story inspires and motivates you, as the reader, to sympathize or empathize with the writer. Connecting with another person's story can spark your desire to walk in your purpose. There's no greater joy than finding someone who wants to achieve the same goals as you.

Throughout my educational career, I became adaptable to social media. I learned how to connect with people with the same passion for education as I did. One of my principals at the time introduced me to the platform Twitter. As an educator new to social media, learning the techniques of Twitter allowed me to share and gain classroom ideas from other educators who did not live in the same area. The power of social media, if used with good intent, can help in a way that inspires one's career, learning, growth, or daily life. When you become inspired to do something or want to achieve something, you unleash a power deep within you. A passion that is stimulating and will motivate those of interest.

Just like social media, sometimes listening to a motivational speaker or even the lyrics to a song can remind a person of the calling and gifts they can share with the world. Words speak to empower, whether you speak them or listen to others, and they can empower you to reflect on your purpose. That said, having an inner circle of people who cheers and encourages is imperative for a support team. For me, I needed to have people praying and motivating me to continue my journey in education. As things became more challenging, I needed to hear more of their words of affirmation to help me persevere.

Having those people in my circle was beneficial to me, but at the same time, I've learned that I was a benefit to them as well. When someone is in your circle, being an encourager, everyone will reap the harvest you will plant. Those people I have listed as a part of my encouragement team had invested interest in my purpose and how I decided to play out my calling. They are my advisory support when going through those bumps and detours of my journey. Seeking and adhering to their counseling gave me the strength I sometimes lacked. For most people, that support team may come from a mother, father, brother, sister, cousin, husband, or wife. Having a group of people who believe in your mission will be those rooted deeply in your harvest. Every person should have at least three people who serve as roots in their lives. Those rooted companionships will never wither away, especially when you are going through a storm or a drought.

When dealing with personal issues or making career choices, you may notice that certain people you thought were a part of your circle are no longer supportive as you expected. If those people are not supporting you, they are not as like-minded as you. You want to get rid of those people as quickly as you can. They are weeds, a plant that is not valued and tends to choke out more desirable plants. When you see those weeds growing in your harvest, remove them immediately!

Sowing seeds in a seasonable environment will benefit you and those who will prosper from your harvest. Adjoining yourself with people with a common interest can make your purpose more enjoyable and less aggressive. When you have supportive friends on the same or similar journey as you, you can both speak and understand each other's language.

Only some people in your surroundings can process your journey and the goals you have set. For example, my husband is one of my dearest friends. A friend to whom I can express most of the concerns I have encountered. We have been childhood friends since the fifth grade and started dating in our junior year in high school. He is my forever sweetheart. And we have had many talks about many different topics, but one topic that can be worn out is the talk about daily work. Yes, your spouse can be very supportive in your career or help when needed to reduce your workload. Still, nothing beats having a good girlfriend to chit-chat about everyday life's ups and downs, especially concerning the competence of career work.

Being a classroom teacher for the last five years has pros and cons. There were moments when I just needed to vent my frustrations. And having another teacher with similar concerns was the best person for me to console.

But on the other hand, the dynamic conversations we would have were very therapeutic. So, we started calling it the "Teacher Talk." A talk where only teachers would understand the language in which one spoke. It always amused me how a group of teachers can talk for hours and hours about the same topic, and no one gets bored.

Every Friday after work, I would hang out with a group of teachers who taught different grade levels than myself. After work, we would meet up at this restaurant called Willies.

We later began to call it our "spot." It was our spot to decompress from a week of work and enjoy each other's company. It was our sacred safe place, and we were regulars, sitting at the same table every week. For most people, having a spot to go weekly to unwind or chit-chat about everyday life is a much-needed spot. Sometimes that spot can be a restaurant, a family member's house, or a neighbor's back patio. It could also be a dedicated time in your day when you are journaling about the week. Whatever soothes you from a long day or week of work is an excellent mechanism for you to distress and reflect. I recommend you get into a routine if you don't have an outlet. It can change your life and make you more social and applicable.

FAITHFULNESS

When Friday rolled around, we knew it would be a good day. We would look forward to that day to talk about our week, the students, other teachers, the curriculum, the school, and even the upcoming professional developments we were "required" to attend. But most of all, we would reflect on how we were making a difference and what we could do better to be that teacher who changes lives. Yes, I'll admit we had moments when we wanted to throw in the towel, give up and even change careers. We were perturbed by the local and state government's constant changes in education reform regarding standardized testing, disciplinary policies, classroom sizes, and other hot topics.

There were situations when we shared tears of disappointment due to unforeseen circumstances and the many drawbacks of promises made by different stakeholders. We looked forward to Fridays because we knew we could've counted on a good talk with friends who shared the same goal.

Having someone or a group of people to talk with is a healthy form of communication and is essential to a human's well-being. Letting out your inner thoughts, whether venting or chatting, reduces stress while making you feel closer to others and providing a sense of belonging. It is a suitable coping mechanism to purge your frustration, disappointments, and any unsettled troubles that may bother you. Besides, you never know the impact your story might have on healing another person's sorrow.

We, as human beings, were not created to be alone in life. Regardless of your current situation, it has been known that working with other individuals, whether collaborating on a given project or being a part of a team to conquer a win, is a part of life's journey. Many teachers, including myself, wanted to be superheroes at some point in our careers. Having those special powers meant I could save a child from any vulnerable situation in which they couldn't protect themselves. But I realized that even superheroes have a team to help them accomplish a given task. When walking in your true purpose, don't try to walk it alone. Even if you try as much as possible to prove you can do this alone, your strength will eventually deplete.

Isolation can be daunting and lonely. In a recent book I read called, *Kids Deserve It*, written by Todd Nesloney and Adam Welcome, there was a whole chapter about not living on an island. The book states: "...if you want to create that spark, you have to get off the island and start collaborating. The good news is that you can choose whom to connect and collaborate with – and they don't have to be within the walls of your building."[12]. Don't isolate yourself on an island by yourself; instead, invest in others with the same interest and positive spirit to do great things.

In the previous chapters, I mentioned that I have two sisters, one passed away in 2000 due to a tragic auto accident, and the other serves as the eldest of my siblings. Since my sister's passing, my other sister, LaKisha, and I have grown a stronger sister bond. Our bond as sisters is a connected relationship that is infrangible and irreplaceable. Just as I would have those "teacher talk" moments with my colleagues, I had similar talks with my sister. When you have a sister talk, you dive into a complex conversation that will stir your spirit. Sister talk does not necessarily mean you have to be conversing with your biological sister. The word sister means the other person truly knows everything about you to where they know your thoughts and see your heart. It's a more profound connection than just

---

[12] Kids Deserve It, by Todd Nesloney and Adam Welcome

THE SEVENTH FRUIT

biological. A person's words can either tear you apart or lift you. But having someone to share your thoughts, concerns, excitement, and silliness can be fulfilling because someone listens and shows genuine interest in your thoughts. Speaking with my sister more frequently brought awareness that I was not alone. Regardless of who was talking, myself or my sister, the other person served as an active listener. As the Bible states, we have two ears and one mouth for a reason.[13] The Bible also speaks about blessings and cursing coming from the same tongue.[14] People's words have power and movement in them. I have learned what I speak about to others can impact negative or positive outcomes. Therefore, I make it a mindful awareness to remain humble when speaking life over death in any situation. My motto is to **speak to empower, not to devour.** You must be cautious about the words and life you will inspire or cast sorrow on. Next time you find yourself in a center conversation, let your next "sister talk" conversation be inspirational. An uplifting word of affirmation that will change any life.

---

[13] Proverbs 25:11-12
[14] James 3:10

Note to Self-Reflect:

If you are entering a new chapter, career, or personal life, find good, faithful friends who will lift you through your journey. The general rule is to find or discover two or three rooted friends that will have your back no matter how the wind may blow. They will be rooted and grounded with you for life. Those people will not be judgmental but honest enough to let you know when you are wrong and heading in the right direction. They will also be there for you in your highs along with your lows. You will encounter many good people as you continue to grow in your calling. But note not everyone will be a friend or a good person to rely on. Some people might be friendly to you simultaneously, telling you things you want to hear while not having your best interest at heart. When you notice those patterns, ask God for wisdom to show you who your real friends are. A distrust friend can sometimes serve as an enemy who can be deceitful and be disguised in sheep's clothing[15]. These people can pretend to be your friend while wishing for failure in your life.

---

[15] Matthew 7:15

Be cautious when you do run into those types of people.

Let's stop to make a list of people you consider a part of your circle. Get a piece of paper and write down the people who have empowered you to be a better person.

Think about this for a moment. Examining the people, you have in your life that you call a friend or use as a support system is essential. But before you start to list their names, I want you to recall those special moments when they strengthened you in your darkest time. To help you analyze this assignment a little deeper, I want you to look at the word "empowerment." What root word do you see? If you answer "power," then you are correct. Now, with the word "power" in mind, list those who have powered you to become a better person. Receiving the strength from the support team to overcome self-doubt can lead to personal empowerment for yourself. This type of empowerment will make you stronger and more confident in making positive decisions and force you to take action that will bring you closer to achieving your goal and ambitions.

FAITHFULNESS

Whoever you listed as a friend, make sure they can relate to your story. Your story is too important for others to take as a joke.

My group of teacher friends each taught different grade levels, had different students, strived for different position levels as an educator, and continued their education either by working on a master's or doctorate. We all were at different places/levels in our journey. All our stories were different, but we supported each other and listened. Sometimes, the listening part might be the answer to what you were seeking. Wisdom will teach you when to speak.

Have you ever surrounded yourself with people who are just like you? How about people that are entirely different from you? Most people tend to gravitate to those with the same interests as themselves. Similarities can be helpful because you can empathize with that person more deeply. But is it always healthy to stay connected with people with the same similarities? How do you challenge yourself to learn about other indifferences if you say yes? Do you indulge in conversations with people who do not look like you? Diversity is what we live in—a world where we can learn from everyone, whether we agree with them or not. I'm very thankful for the many people that have come in and out of my lifespan.

You will also encounter many friendships along your journey.

Some of those friendships will be seasonal, and some will be a lifetime. Remember, those seasonal friends will only impact your life just for that season. While in that season with those friends, you will cherish those moments you have learned during that relationship and nothing else. There will be no growing or gaining harvest with those friends.

On the contrary, those lifetime friendships will not be seasoning friendships, and those friends will be in your life forever. They will become your anchor friends, not withering away when things get tough. They will be with you through all the seasons of your life, constantly growing with you. You will find no greater joy than seeing a friend prosper just as you thrive.

For those who don't believe in having a support team, let me be the first to tell you that you will need other people in your life! A group of people who believe in your vision and who are ready to walk out of your mission statement. Please do not be fooled by your selfish knowledge and think you are the only one that can save the world and change lives. There's a reason why God sent HIS disciples in teams of two. The Bible says that when two or more come together in HIS name, things (spiritually speaking) start to happen. There is also truth to this statement: more extraordinary things will happen when two or more human beings come together to conquer a given vision.

If you are one of those, who choose to be secretive and less passionate about their purpose. Then it may stem from a sense of fear, causing you to be less emotional and inspirational. It could be fear of being rejected by others, fear of failure, or even fear that you may be successful. Whatever you fear, I'm here to tell you not to let fear get in your way of living a purposeful and powerful life.

Tell yourself you are a person with a particular calling in your life—a calling where fear is not a part of the agenda. Your calling will require you to act and make moves that will impact the lives of others. Your calling will make you stronger, more confident, and capable of self-control, which will lead you to a fruitful life. When acting in your calling, surround yourself with other fearless, empowering, confident, strong-minded people

THE SEVENTH FRUIT

who will help you through the next steps of your journey.

Believing in yourself and others shows maturity in how fruitful you are becoming. It shows your true character of wanting to see others WIN in life. When you become excited to see others grow and prosper, God will give you more great opportunities to achieve.

Gentleness

The Eighth Fruit

Chapter 8:

GENTLENESS will lead to Greatness.

"Let your gentleness be evident to all"
—Philippians 4:5

"Congratulations, it's a boy!" were the words that came from my doctor's mouth as I had just given birth to my firstborn baby. It was September 25th, 1998. My husband and I were so excited to be new parents; our parents would be grandparents for the first time as well. Joy and love filled the room as I held my baby for the first time. After being under anesthesia for numerous hours, I was a little out of it but still awake to know that I just gave birth to a healthy, beautiful baby, who we named Daylon Javon.

Children are indeed a blessing from up above. When Daylon was born, he was so sweet and fragile. As a mother, I wanted to ensure I handled him with extra care by being as gentle as possible, ensuring he was not in harm or pain. My job was to protect and be the overbearing mother who is extremely safeguarding to her child as much as possible. After all, he was my first and only child then, and I had no clue what to do as a new parent. Have you ever wondered why parents take extra caution with their firstborn? What makes the firstborn so unique that we as parents apply specific rules or demands when caring for him/she? The Bible would talk about the blessing bestowed on the 1st born, especially if it were a male. It has been known and studied by some scholars that a firstborn child carries a special gift of blessing, especially in biblical times. With this being true, then it is important, as parents, to protect their child even more because of the high blessings upon one's life.

For this reason, most parents tend to overly bear their firstborn baby. But by the time most parents get to the second or third child, all those precautions of overly bearing for a child go straight out the window. The way a parent handles each child changes from baby to baby. This scenario is similar to when a person is starting something new in their life. Just as a mother who holds, protects, and nourishes her newborn for the first time, so will you be with the calling God has entrusted you with.

Once I received my Master's in Education Leadership, I took on a leadership role as an Instructional Specialist. At this time, I had relocated to a different school district and was working in the same community I was living in. My new role was to observe and guide teachers in ensuring they were teaching the curriculum with fidelity. Since this was a new role and being at a new school district, I wanted to be gentle, handling every situation with precaution.

Not knowing what to expect from the teachers, I was very cautious about my timing and delivery when observing their lessons. Since I was no longer working directly with kids, I had to reframe my mindset on how I would approach the learning habits of those teachers under my leadership. My audience had now shifted from kids to adults. Therefore, my delivery on how I would reach them also had to shift. When you grow in your life, career-wise or personally, you will find yourself speaking differently based on your target audience. You must credibly mature yourself to capture people's hearts and make a difference in what you are trying to portray. Students have open mindsets and are willing to do as their teacher instructs. Some adults, not all, have a fixed mindset, making it difficult to see a change positively. This new role gave me challenges I had to overcome if I wanted to keep fulfilling my purpose.

As stated before, growth is a good thing. No matter your age, race, or economic status, you, too, can achieve some type of growth in your life. That said, as an individual looking to be fruitful, I had to brand in my mind never to stop learning and growing. Each day I was committed to learning more about my strengths and capacity to grow as a person. The human brain keeps producing electrons as long as the brain is being challenged with new information or recurring information. When presented with this leadership role, I knew I would be challenged by those who now looked at me as being the expert. The person with all the "right" answers and solutions to every problem. That was my assumption, the expectation from others looking outside onto my new role. Since all eyes were on me in this leadership role, the weight of the position was starting to get heavy. Specific decision-making challenged me to keep my gentle persona while facing complex tasks. As a new person, I didn't want to be rude or seem insensitive to those I was establishing a working relationship. Once again, I started questioning my decision-making and whether I was the right person for the job. Insecure began to seep in again, and I found myself back at the beginning asking God if this was the right move. God had reassured me regardless of my career movement and resilience to growth, my calling to educate was still a part of my purpose. When you are called to do something, you will have opportunities to grow in that calling. No matter your challenges, showing benignity to others will serve its purpose.

At this point, I was no longer in my comfort zone. The school culture was different from what I was accustomed to; now, I was a part of the leadership team versus a grade-level team. All the work behind the scenes I had put in from my previous campus finally paid out. I was finally using the knowledge and skills I gained from my last school/district. Being under outstanding leadership is imperative when moving up into a leadership position. You can't be a leader if you are unwilling to learn and grow with the team you are guiding. If your leadership team or principal is not ready to take risks by advocating for the team or school, please find another leader willing to guide others. My new current principal was known as a great #LeadLearner who modeled her expectations. Especially when it came to maintaining a school culture where every student had an opportunity to learn in a safe environment, she was always willing to push the team and staff to grow, learn, and take chances for our students.

We participated in multiple book studies, shared sessions, and many professional developments, allowing us to challenge ourselves as educators. Her motto was #bethemodel. And she meant it. Let's just say she had a nosebleed expectation.

At first, getting used to the new role was very challenging. But eventually, it started to feel natural to me. Your calling will feel natural to you as well. When it does, you will know you are on the right path. New opportunities will be given for you to grow and mature. My new role at this point was to work with teachers willing to invest in curriculum growth for their students. By doing so, I had to be accustomed to learning the curriculum for all grade levels (Pre K -5). I had to familiarize myself with teachers' different learning styles in their lessons to ensure all students were achieving. My role also included looking closely at the school campus testing data to find the root cause and solving problems that would close the gap for a better outcome performance rate. When allowed to lead, it is important to be a servant to all—every person under your leadership matters. The accountability level will arise as the expectation level increases. Just as at the beginning of my teacher days, I now had to invest twice as much in ensuring I was fully prepared to accommodate what was being asked of me. Which means working past the usual hours and putting in time on the weekends. If you are serious about your personal or career growth, you will invest the extra time in yourself and those around you or under your leadership/ guidance. People willing to lead and take a stand will always surpass what is expected of their job expectations. This level of commitment shows that you are genuinely invested in seeing the harvest you are a part of. Your dedication and patience to planting and watching seeds grow will show your compassion and gentleness about others. When God sees how much you have been reaping your harvest, HE will give you more great opportunities to oversee. HE will entrust you to be even more of a great leader to many more people who will come your way.

In my four-year seasonal time as an Instructional Specialist, I had the pleasure of working with over fifty plus teachers, ranging from zero years of experience to over 20 years of dedicated services. The impact these teachers made on their students' lives was remarkable. The achievement level scores soared and remained in the high percentile throughout the school year, receiving exemplary distinctions within the district. I was very grateful and humbled to witness these teachers' growth while in my leadership's presence. Some eventually moved into leadership roles, such as Curriculum Coaches, Technology Specialists, Math Interventionists, Blended Learning cohort teachers, and Instructional Specialists.

Leadership is a huge title, and it's a responsibility to lead. Only some people will be called for this position. You must know your part and how to

THE EIGHTH FRUIT

play your role which affects those around you. Some people may be called just to serve and not lead, which is okay. Your service is just as important as any other title. To be a leader, you must first serve. Even while leading, you must continue to serve. That's the only way you will grow into leadership or become better at leading. Authentic leadership starts with being a servant to others.

Just as giving birth to a newborn baby for the first time or purchasing your first home, you too will have that first-time feeling of excitement when you discover your purpose in life. It will be an "aha" moment of the sudden discovery of gifts and talents you've had deep inside your spirit. First, you will want to work with diligence. This will allow you to put in that extra effort to ensure everything goes smoothly and well. Second, you will want to lead with greatness. Therefore, you will invest more in resources, time, and other people as you grow in your calling. When you have arrived in this position, be mindful of all the other fruits you have sewn leading up to this moment.

Remember to let your gentleness be evident to all.

Note to Self-Reflect:

When you are new at doing something, whether being a parent for the first time or your first job, you must be as gentle and diligent as possible. The excitement of being introduced to achieving something new will make you feel the need to take your time and cause fewer errors. Think of when you have been in a situation where you wanted to take your precious time and ensure things were handled with care. You know the moments of dotting all the "I's" and crossing all the "T's." Do you have a memory in mind? If so, then were you successful in accomplishing that new task? When put in a position to make a first impression, the pressure of succeeding can sometimes become overwhelming. No one wants to feel like a failure on the first try.

To be gentle with something or someone is to be even-tempered, humble, and compassionate toward others or the subject matter. Showing an attitude filled with gentleness is excellent, not just at the beginning when starting something new but at every aspect of your life. When those opportunities arrive your way, accept them with an open heart, cuddling and nourishing them as much as possible. These opportunities are a part of the labor you have been reaping. God will give you those opportunities because he entrusted you with the assignment. He has seen your due diligence to sow seeds in many areas, not just in the field you are in.

If you can lead in life, then lead with a gentle heart. Be kind, humble, and, most importantly, compassionate. A peaceful person makes no abrupt movements or declarations. But instead, they are courteous, polite, and soothing to be around.

When I was allowed to be a part of a leadership team, a team who led the school curriculum and instruction department, I had to remind myself of how it was when I was a classroom teacher. Leadership came after I served as a teacher. I needed to know where I started and where I was going. The same goes for you and your journey. Your journey to impact others will be led by your service. How you affect those around you and those you will eventually lead will determine how great of a leader you will become. Let your intentions and expectations of the role embody what authentic leadership means. You will only be fruitful if you plant true, natural seeds, not placebo seeds. True fruitfulness comes from sources that have your best interest at heart.

When planting seeds that will benefit the lives of others, you will have to cultivate the soil to see the growth sprouts produced by enabling yourself to continue to learn and grow while nurturing the field at hand. For example, when I moved into leadership status, I had to rethink differently from being a teacher. The audience I had invested in for the past six years had changed from students to adults. How I operated as a teacher differed from the function I needed as an Instructional Specialist in a leadership role. Just as my life changed, so will your life change once you have answered your calling and started to live out your purpose. You will start to rethink, react, and reposition yourself to grow in new ways.

Because of your willingness to move, learn and grow in a different environment, you will become a better, stronger, wiser, and more confident person. You will want to read more, learn more,

THE EIGHTH FRUIT

and reflect more. So, when God gives you your next BIG assignment, you will be ready to take on and bring the fruits you have harvested thus far into planting into your next assignment.

Self-Control

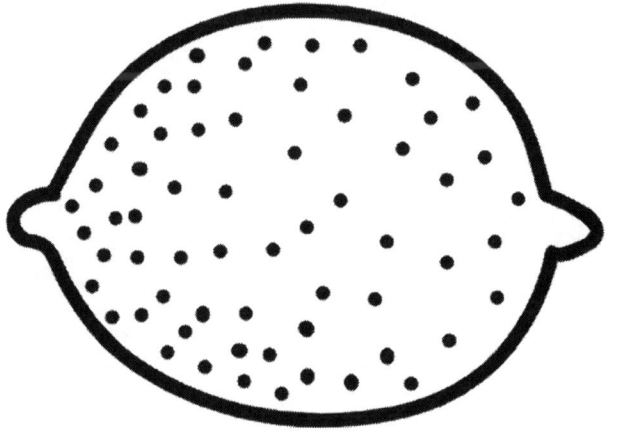

The Ninth Fruit

Chapter 9:

SELF-CONTROL =
Awareness + Reflection

"He who angers you… controls you."

-Proverbs 16:32

Knowledge is Power. Those are words that most people use to feel empowered. But what do these words really mean? To have knowledge is one thing, but to apply it gives it a greater meaning. According to Wikipedia, *knowledge* is a familiarity, awareness, or understanding of someone or something, such as facts, information, descriptions, or skills acquired through experience or education by perceiving, discovering, or learning. When you are at the height of your awareness, you have the intellect to accomplish big and powerful things. That's when you feel most powerful in influencing the behavior of others or the course of events.

SELF-CONTROL

While studying in grad school to receive my master's degree, I encountered a lot of reading and reflecting. The reading part was to gain knowledge of the information needed for my study subject. And the reflection was for me to think about how to make what I read fit into my life. It was more of the application part I would apply in my life. There were also countless hours of book studying, numerous intense case studies, and many vocabulary words I had to remember and take part in. The program lasted for about 18 months, followed by a three-month internship. Much work, time, and effort were put into receiving this degree.

Most importantly, having the self-discipline to finish the program was essential to me. Once completed, I now had the knowledge and power to further my education career because of this degree's necessity.

The intensity of completing this program in a certain amount of time frame, along with my other daily duties like being a mom, wife, teacher, etc., caused a lot of pressure on my emotional being. There were moments when I wanted to put my studies on hold until I had more time to focus and complete the program. But the way the program was designed was most suitable for me to obtain during that time. This was an opportunity where I had to push myself to get this chapter of my life moving. If not, then it would have never gotten done. Some people thought I was insane for taking on such a big project like this while still attending to daily life duties. They told me that it was a waste of time and money. And I should be focusing on my family since they are my top priority. The naysayers also told me that the only thing I would get out of this was a piece of paper that said completed. Those words made me second-guess myself and wonder if this was all I would walk away with. Instead of letting those words get to me, I had to focus on the big picture and the positive outcome this degree would bring me. Doing so taught me how to block out other people's negative presumptions about my life. I knew finishing what I started was way more important than what others had to say. The word "complete" on that paper had a deeper meaning than just its print. For me to be completed meant I have mastered something I first dreamed of, and now it has been accomplished. It meant I pushed myself to finish a task that seemed impossible initially. I had turned a possibility into a reality. This type of mastery takes self-discipline, which is

SELF-CONTROL

the ability to control one's feelings and overcome one's weaknesses.

For that, I was very grateful for the completion of this program. During this period, I needed to continue working on my professional growth and personal spiritual journey. Therefore, daily devotionals and academic readings were significant to my well-being and personal growth. The power of reading, reflecting, and challenging the mind daily can bring powerful awareness to anyone's self-being. Because of this routine that I chose to implement in my life gave me the self-confidence I needed as a person to stand up to those naysayers who couldn't grasp the magnitude of my purpose and calling for others. When other people don't understand your life purpose, they will try to corrupt your mind and make you think less of yourself. Because of my discipline to self-reflect on daily occurrences, I began to learn more about myself versus hearing others' thoughts about me. I have learned not to give others the power to speak negatively about the life God has appointed for me. Therefore, I needed to have self-control over my own life. When you commit to reading and reflecting on your personal growth, you, too, can have self-control over your own life.

Educators teach those in second grade "how to read." That way, by the time they get to third grade, they will "read to learn." Just as reading is fundamental for children, so is it essential for adults. Reading and reflecting are two critical skills that should be a central motivation in someone's daily life.

In some cases, most people will reflect daily about the decisions they made or would have made, but they will not take time to read as often as they should. For most people, it is easier to reflect or think about their actions than to pick up a book and read about how to improve their behavior. Applying the mind to do something physically is considered a "mind over matter" action. Everyone will want to demonstrate this type of mind frame at some point.

Just as a child seeks to read books of interest, you too will want to read books or topics that will interest your calling and purpose in life. Once you begin to reflect on your reading, your mind will become conscious of what you can do. The neurons in your brain will cause it to fire up and send off chemical and electrical signals to help you to understand the words and their meaning. This is how you get actual knowledge and power over

SELF-CONTROL

your own learning. It is a type of self-awareness that only you can control. Once you have it, it's up to you to implement it and share it with others.

Over the past few years, when I served on the leadership team at one of the two elementary schools. My then-principal, whom she referred to herself as the #LeadLeaner of the campus, would have the leadership team read numerous books and discuss applying the readings to our everyday work life. The purpose of reading those books wasn't just to reflect on how to be a better person but how we can lead others to become self-sufficient in their own learning. Reading those books and reflecting on the content made me realize how important it is to grow daily in my professional workspace and personal life.

Even though I had a few completed degrees and qualifications, those accomplishments didn't signify that my journey had ended. It wasn't the "end-all" result of my life. Sometimes it depends on how you look at a word. The word "completed" can be seen as an indication to start something new or keep adding to what you have created.

Just as we, individuals, grow and become wiser with age, so will our purpose in life. Expiration dates should never be put on your purpose and calling. As long as you breathe and have life in you, you should continue to nurture the gifts you were meant to share with the world and others who surround you. Don't allow the word "completed" to be the final print of the last pages you read. Don't fool yourself into thinking that's a stopping point in life. Your life of living is more than just seeing the finish line.

Note to Self-Reflect:

When you set your mind to pursue something that you know will benefit yourself and others, you are activating your purpose and calling. You are taking actions that you can control and are capable of doing. Don't allow naysayers to tell you what you can or cannot do. Be in control of your own thoughts. The thoughts of what you can be or do in life. Learn more about yourself through daily scripture reading and reflection. Doing so will discover your likes, dislikes, strengths, weaknesses, and other skills you may not know. Remember that everyone has a purpose, a calling, and a gift to share with the world. And your purpose, calling, and gifts won't be something you can't bear. God will always give you the strength and necessary tools to succeed in your mission. You won't ever have to question if what you are doing is the right thing or not. My mom always said, "you will know when something is meant for you because the seed will have your name on it." Once you find or discover your gift (seed), then set out (plant it) and watch your life transform (grow). Let's take a moment to reflect deeply.

Think of a time when you went through a vast amount of studying, reading, and reflecting on completing a program or assignment you had once started. Have you ever completed that task? If not, then what is it that's keeping you from finishing? For most people, time and money are the two significant factors that can stop them from pursuing a goal. The best way to overcome any fear factor holding you back is first to write down precisely what you want to achieve. Make sure to write a reasonable time frame that will coincide with your current work. For example, I decided to pursue my master's degree while still teaching in the school district. The time frame of going back to school went perfectly as I was already in the field of education. It didn't burden my learning abilities because I was familiar with the content subject at hand. If you are considering returning to school to pursue a career you have not yet indulged in, set up a support team to help you along your journey. Surround yourself with like-minded people who have the same interest in you. Get connected with people who will help ease your journey as you begin something new.

In the meantime, you should read materials that will help your journey. While reading and reflecting, start thinking about how you will apply the knowledge you've gained to your or another's life. Start allowing your mind to explore possibilities of what your life will look like once you have completed that task, degree, or assignment. And stay away from naysayers and negative thoughts that will derail you from achieving your goals.

Once you discover who you are, then you will have the power to stay in control of your own actions. Remember that life is about 10% of what happens to you and 90% how you react to it. That being said, you have more control over how you react than what happens to you. When living your best life, you can choose authenticity over others' perceptions and acceptance.

To have self-control over your life, you have to bear the fruits that will lead you to a life of productivity. A productive life is full of wisdom, understanding, power, and prosperity. And when you do, you will see the harvest of your fruitfulness.

For those who are looking forward to retirement, then think about what's in store for your next journey? Your purpose in life will not have a 401k retirement plan. Even though retirement is the action of leaving one's job and ceasing to work.

However, your life will not be subject to retirement when you live a purposeful life on earth. Your purpose and calling will only end when you have reached death. That statement may sound harsh, but there is truth to it. So, whether you are on the verge of retirement or completing a huge task, I want you to consider your last big career accomplishment. Once you had finished the job, was there another opportunity presented to you to be a part of? If not, what about a job you most likely failed at? Did you get another chance to correct the mistakes that caused you to fail? Some people may say they have never made any mistakes or had regrets and that everything that happened was meant to happen. Do you think that's a true statement? If so, how would you argue that statement? For me, I can see that being a true statement. However, I am sure we all have moments where we wish we could have done things differently or taken a different path in life. Either way, many of you have been blessed with opportunities to make life better.

Every day you wake up, you are allowed to start over. Each new day comes with new adventures, dreams, innovations, and ways to make the day cheerful and purposeful.

When was the last time (besides the COVID-19 pandemic) that you found yourself in a place of silence? A place where no one else was around and you could self-reflect on your life decisions. If you say you never had a quiet moment to read and reflect on your goals, aspirations, and purpose for living, then you are robbing yourself of opportunities to make your life more productive and fruitful.

God wants you to be fruitful. And HE will give you moments to self-reflect on your purpose, calling, and gifts for you to use.

THE FRUIT OF THE SPIRIT

Love Peace
Patience Kindness
Joy Goodness
Faithfulness Self Control Gentleness

Living A Fruitful Life

Chapter 10:

You are *FRUITFUL*.

An apple a day keeps the doctor away. Those were the words my grandmother used to tell me as a kid. I never really grasped the meaning of what she was trying to say at the time. But as I got older, I wondered, what if that statement is true? What if you can eat all the suitable fruits and vegetables and never have to see a doctor for any health issues? How amazing that would be. If that statement holds any truth, I will immediately start a garden in my backyard to grow as many fruits and vegetables as possible to appease my diet to a healthy lifestyle.

Growing up, I always admired people who enjoyed gardening and grew their produce. It is something about growing your own food that is inspiring and brings comfort to know where it came from. I knew starting a garden would consume lots of labor, time, effort, and resources to get it going. I would have to educate myself on the different seed types and plan the timing for a productive harvest. Most people believe you will live longer if you eat organic foods. I'm convinced that eating healthy foods like fruits and vegetables in your daily life might prevent certain illnesses in your body. However, I'm not too confident that what you eat will give you a life of longevity.

On the other hand, I am sure that the words you speak from your mouth and heart will be (seeds) planted into the lives of others that will live for a long time. Those seeds of affirmation planted into the lives of others will impact the health of how a person will live.

I believe every person on this earth has been given seeds of life to be planted into another's life. Whether those seeds are of good nature, it is up to the producer (you) to choose the seeds for their harvest. Some of those seeds will produce fruitfulness while other seeds will wither off. You will know if your seed has withered based on how it looks. It will become dry, shriveled, and eventually deteriorate into death. God will always give each individual a choice in life on how they want to plant their harvest.

With the choice in your hand, you can begin to live in your purpose, knowing you have the power to produce life and death.

Once you have made that choice, you will be ready to walk into your calling. But before you activate your purpose and answer your calling, you must first take a vow for the actions that you have encountered.

When I came of age where I could've made decisions without any guidance, I knew it was up to me to apply all that I'd learned from my parents, grandparents, and those who were a part of my village. When I married my husband, a childhood friend, my commitment to him was to be his better half, soul mate, and wife. When I became a mother, my responsibility was to love, adorn and raise my kids with good ethical morals that would stay with them throughout their young adolescence into adulthood. When I chose my career in education, my allegiance was to dedicate myself to learning, growing, and sharing knowledge with my students, colleagues, community, and other stakeholders who were a part of my network.

The point is that every person has been given a choice in life on how they want to live the life

God gave them. In making those choices, you have the power to create an enjoyable and fruit-bearing life.

As I mentioned in chapter 4, we live in a world where everything is a fingertip away. We get things done within seconds to produce fast results. Our patience to tolerate "timing" has been minimized to a "right now" moment. Just like those seeds God has given you to plant, some things in life cannot be rushed or quickly developed. The growth and development of your calling will be reflected in the seeds planted in your heart. It is the process, which is timing, of when you will see the essential growth of your harvest coming into maturity.

As a science teacher, I have always enjoyed teaching and demonstrating how the life cycle works. In a generic life cycle, you have four stages: introduction, growth, maturity, and decline. Those are the basics of a life cycle. However, there is a seed, sprout, small plant, and adult plant in a plant life cycle. The beginning stage of a plant, also known as the germination stage, is where the plant starts to form. It's the process of something coming into existence and developing after being in a state of no movement. This is a similar scenario in one's life. We are born into this world, raised by those who care, taught by those who educate, and then off to live an adult life. In our adult life, we start to impact others around us. This is the stage where your purpose and calling bring meaning to those around you, whether in the community or the world you live in.

Like any other livable thing, your life is a cycle that will come with an expiration date. You are born, you will live, and then you will die. The seeds you have in you will be the seeds to begin the cycle again. Because no one knows how much time is allotted to their life, many have asked, when is the right time to walk in my purpose or how do I know if I'm walking in my purpose? First, you must acknowledge that your life has purpose and meaning. Once you have declared by taking your first breath daily, you are given a reason to live out your purpose.

Every single person in life has a purpose for living. Being on this earth is not just about existing until you can't exist anymore. There is so much to life than just being here. Yes, you will wake up and do the daily routines of eating, going to work, paying bills, entertaining family, and friends, celebrating different holidays and occasions, attending certain functions, and then off to bed just to repeat the day. While repeating the day, you will be given opportunities to replay the moments where you can impact other individuals trying to find their purpose in life. You will be given opportunities to harvest those seeds so that you can replant them into the next person. When walking in your purpose, you leave footprints that will pave the way for others to know there's much more in life than just existing.

With age comes wisdom, just as ignorance is bliss. Only you will have the willpower to determine if you want to live in wisdom or be ignorant of life. You will have the final call if you want to leave a legacy behind with purpose and meaning or just to live a day-to-day life hoping something good will come your way. My favorite book in the Bible is the Book of James (New Testament). It consists of five chapters that have some life-value lessons. I'm a firm believer that 'faith without work is dead". It means you can hope, pray, and believe in something, but without any actions behind it, or any work put forth, it is void (empty). To have a purpose in life is to believe in a greater good, an act of kindness that will produce greater interest and more acts of kindness among others that will spread throughout this world. To be fruitful is to plant seeds of love, joy, peace, patience, kindness, goodness, faithfulness, gentleness, and self-control. To be withered is death which is the opposite of fruitful that can produce hate, sadness, havoc, anxiety, rudeness, bad, mistrust, roughness, and out of control.

If you enjoy seeing the rainbow after the storm, you must be willing to endure the rain. Without rain, you won't be able to live a fruitful life. And you cannot be fruitful if you are living in a drought. Our mundane daily routines and lifestyle can lead us to a droughtful or "dry" life. You must stay encouraged, positioning yourself around people who care enough to see you succeed. You need a village that will cheer you on while running your race. Even when you fall, because you WILL fall in life, you still need that support system to help you get back on track. Surround yourself with people that have a driven purpose for their lives. People who will not be afraid to tell you when you are off track but will help keep you accountable.

Much of this book is dedicated to my early career as an educator. I have shared my story and journey on how my students, colleagues, friends, and family helped me define my purpose and calling. My goal consists of living a fruitful life and my calling to teach and educate. My call to action is to continually plant seeds of prosperity, inspiration, and the willingness to pass on love and kindness to others so they may also be productive into the lives of the next person/generation.

Note to Self-Reflect:

When reflecting on your life, do you see your life as being fruitful? Before answering that question. Think of what seeds you have planted that will produce good fruits in another life. Here is a list of those fruits: love, joy, peace, patience, kindness, goodness, faithfulness, gentleness, and self-control. Which fruits are you currently producing? And which ones do you still need to work on? If you listed more fruits to work on versus what you are producing, then maybe it's time to check the harvest you are reaping. Those crops may be withered fruits that hinder you from living an enjoyable life.

Fast forward to your future and consider how you will leave your legacy. How do you want to be remembered? If you are a parent, have you taken the time to show your children how to be fruitful and do what's right in life? If you have no kids, then what about a friend? Have you helped a friend in time of need or consoled the elderly? What about those who are widows? Think about your deeds and what you have passed on that will continue to prosper in those around you.

Remember, the seeds you are seeking to plant are already within you. The words that come out of your mouth, the innermost thoughts you ponder, your demeanor, and the body language you give off to others. That's your seed(s). The million-dollar question is: When will you start planting those seeds? Are you going to plant them once you become a wife, mother, or career woman? Will you plant them once you discover your purpose and calling in life? When will you define the right time to start growing your seeds?

Let's stop, pause, and reflect.

This is a pivotal time in your life when I want you to stop and think about the harvest you are currently in. Do you feel like you are in the self-control of your life? Are you waiting on a particular season to plant your seed? Maybe you are waiting for a loved one to experience that moment with. Or perhaps you are waiting on that career to have some financial resources. But does it cost anything to plant a seed? Your life is based

YOU ARE FRUITFUL

on time, and time is of the essence when it comes to living your life. So let me ask you one more time. Who or what are you waiting for to start living a purposeful life?

The smallest seed to be recorded in the Bible is a grain of mustard seed. The scriptures tell us that having faith the size of a mustard seed means you have hope to live a life of prosperity. With that exact grain of hope is believing that nothing is impossible for God who lives in you[16]. All you need is a little hope to know you are purposefully made, and God designed and created you for HIS will to become the woman you are meant to be. Start today, walking in your purpose daily. And you will see goodness and mercy following you wherever you may go. You will be fully shielded by God's protection and the comfort of HIS Holy Spirit. You will walk confidently, knowing your purpose, calling, and gifts in life. When you know your purpose in life and have live up to it, you can conquer anything that comes your way. You will be a fruit bearer, bearing all fruits. Because you are FRUITFUL!

---

[16] Luke 1:37

Conclusion

I titled this book, She's Bearing All Fruits to dig deeper into finding one's purpose and calling. Everyone has a purpose in life. A drive to do good or to do evil. With that being said, each person is born with a given name and with rules/guidelines which are provided by their parents, community, and society to abide by. They use the information passed down to structure and live their best lives. But as individuals get older, they can decide how they want to live. Discovering your purpose and understanding why you exist is vital to your being. You don't have to be a scholar or have a hidden gift that makes you more relevant or unique than the next person. All you need is willpower and faith to believe you are destined for greatness.

The good thing about God's daily grace is that you can change your outcome if you do not like how life is going for you. It starts with a simple prayer, asking God for wisdom and understanding.

It begins with writing out your thoughts and creating a vision of where you want to be or what you want to accomplish. It starts in the mind and then to the heart, where there is a burning desire to get it done. It begins with collaborating with others who will support you in your journey, sharing your plans and how you will get there. It begins with installing confidence within, knowing you are worthy of contributing to other people's lives. But as you noticed, it must "begin" somewhere.

When you start something, it means you have to physically do something. It requires some sort of action to get things moving. You can't allow fear or failure to hold you back from making an action that will bring you so much joy. If you fail, then start over. If it didn't work out the first time, reflect and revise what went wrong. If you need to keep pressing the start button until you see progress, keep pushing it.

In those trials and tribulations and cloudy storms, keep planting those seeds of love, joy, peace, patience, kindness, goodness, faithfulness, gentleness, and self-control.

Keep walking into the life that God has created you to live, a bountiful life. If you need to change

CONCLUSION

your shoes based on the situation you might be in, then change them and never stop walking.

This is your time to live your purpose, put on your shoes, and start your race. A race that only you can run. It's time to get up and go on a climb, take a step forward, walk in your calling, and reach for your destiny.

The time has come for you to watch the greatness of your life unfold into a fruitful bountiful journey.

It is harvest time.

She's Bearing All Fruits Highlights

Chapter 1

- When you have genuine compassion for living life on purpose, then nothing will be able to hinder you from seeking out your true calling.
- Remember, your purpose is a special calling that only you can fulfill based on the gifts God has given you.
- When you are self-aware of what you love to do, you will live life more freely.

Chapter 2

- To have no goals or aspirations is to live a droughtful life.
- Remember, a *dream* backed up by a *goal* with steps of a *plan* will eventually become a *reality*.

- Start implementing positive thoughts in your mind knowing you are meant to serve this purpose and that you are the right person for the job.

Chapter 3

- When you are eager for change and success, your mind will not be programmed to a 9-5 work shift.
- Knowing your purpose, answering your calling, and aligning it with what you do daily will change your life forever.
- When you are willing to accept feedback and learn from it, you will want to invest more time and effort into the task given to you.

Chapter 4

- When you are all in, working diligently to accomplish a given goal, you won't have time to compare yourself with others in the same industry.
- Don't be afraid to take that chance when new opportunities are presented.

- Your true purpose in life will not be limited to an "on" and "off" season. Instead, it will be a daily habit of wanting to do greatness in the lives of others.

Chapter 5

- Whatever your title in life, wearing your daily spiritual attire will lead you to a life filled with gratitude.
- These types of clothes are free at no cost and with no taxes added to them. You don't have to pay for delivery or wait for it to be in stock. You just have to be willing to open your heart and mind. Be open to sharing, sending, and receiving the fruits that make life enjoyable.
- You are the only person who can label yourself based on your attitude and how you feel about life.

Chapter 6

- The best time to soar to the next big thing is when you have excelled in your current position.

- Life is beautiful, but that doesn't mean it will always bring beauty.
- Your goal will always be wanting to gain more, so you can give more.

Chapter 7

- Every person should have at least three people who serve as roots in their lives. Those rooted companionships will never wither away, especially when you are going through a storm or a drought.
- Adjoining yourself with people with a common interest can make your purpose more enjoyable and less aggressive.
- An uplifting word of affirmation that will change any life.

Chapter 8

- When you are called to do something, you will have opportunities to grow in that calling.
- To be a leader, you must first serve.
- Leadership is a huge title, and it's a responsibility to lead.

Chapter 9

- When you are at the height of your awareness, you have the intellect to accomplish big and powerful things.
- Expiration dates should never be put on your purpose and calling.
- To have self-control over your life, you have to bear the fruits that will lead you to a life of productivity.

Chapter 10

- The growth and development of your calling will be reflected in the seeds planted in your heart.
- The seeds you have in you will be the seeds to begin the cycle again.
- If you enjoy seeing the rainbow after the storm, you must be willing to endure the rain. Without rain, you won't be able to live a fruitful life.

Endnotes

1. Ann Spangler & Jean E. Syswerda, "Women of the Bible," *A one-year Devotional Study of Women in Scriptures*
2. Seven Christian virtues (2 Peter 1:5)
3. Scripture from Proverbs 31:15-24
4. Gary Chapman, The Five Love Languages
5. Inspirational Quote from Neale Donald Walsch
6. Inspirational Quote from unknown
7. Scripture from Deuteronomy 31:8
8. Inspirational Quote Zen Shin
9. Inspirational Quote by Angela Maiers
10. Scripture from Galatians 5:22
11. Scripture from Ephesians 6:11
12. Kids Deserve It, by Todd Nesloney and Adam Welcome
13. Scripture from Proverbs 25:11-12
14. Scripture from James 3:10
15. Scripture from Matthew 7:15
16. Scripture from Luke 1:37

About the Author

LaDwina Flegeance is an Educator and Entrepreneur who has served in her community for the past two decades. She received her Master's in Educational Leadership at Lamar University & Bachelor of Science from McNeese State University and attended Dallas Theological Seminary. She is deeply invested in her church's community, facilitating several outreach programs, and having served in children's ministry for several years. LaDwina is a huge advocate for public education and has served on numerous committees within her school districts.

LaDwina is the CEO of the Flegeance Insurance Agency, an agency that educates and advises its clients on the wealth of their securities. She is also the founder of *Fruits of HER Labor,* a non-profit organization for women seeking opportunities to create their businesses.

Being an inspiring motivator to others, LaDwina also loves hosting gatherings at her home for family and friends. She enjoys dancing, cooking, and spending quality time on her patio.

Stay Fruitful

Thank you so much for coming on this journey with me. If you feel inspired to live a fruitful life, visit my website TheFruitsofHERLabor.com and text FRUITFUL to 888-840-4492.

Made in the USA
Columbia, SC
12 October 2023